ESSENTIALS OF TOURISM

YAJNA RAJ SATYAL

ADROIT PUBLISHERS
DELHI-110 053

Published by
ADROIT PUBLISHERS
C-8/2, Yamuna Vihar,
Delhi-110 053

ISBN No. : 81-87392-14-2

Edition : First

Price : Rs. 250

Laser Typsetting at :
Nidhi Laser Point,
Shahdara, Delhi-110 032

Printed : Nidhi Enterprises
Delhi-110 032

CONTENTS

FOREWORD

This book has been published the hope that it might be of assistance to those individuals interested in tourism training courses in different travel trade services and hotel management training institutions opened and operating now in the country. For the effective development of the tourist industry a high level of co-operation between the elements of the industry is essential; and to achieve this, leadership and organisation are required. To develop skilled leadership and organisation a well developed man-power is required and those elements are only progressed with the development of vocational institutions throughout the country run by specialized technicians.

Taking into account the establishment of many tourism vocational training institutes in the country, it is necessary now to have some books on the essentials of tourism for the persons interested in this subject. This book is the first of this kind and hope that it will help and assist in imparing knowledge to the participants on the subject. So it has been tried to provide comprehensive treatment of all topics and exhaustive analysis of tourism and its essential elements. It adds valuable references on each case of subjects to make them more easy and simple. The major focus of the book is on the study of tourism in a development context which is more influential for a developing country like ours. It is hoped and believed that this book will eventually be beneficial for the persons interested to learn and acquire knowledge in tourism which is becoming as one of the essential elements of the national economy and is considered as a real "Invisible export".

Author

1

TOURISM IN THE PRESENT WORLD

Tourism is passing through the modern world as a conspicuous activity. Its presence is settled and there has been much relationship with its development at present. It comes into play as the world's largest industry. The tourism industry has made a leading contribution in improving the country's balance of payment and position, to increasing employment opportunities and indirectly towards sustaining overall development efforts. So there has been as much concern with tourism development. Many are of the opinion that tourism is a homogeneous, well-organised, tenacious positive phenomenon. That is why, tourism in the modern world, is characterised by a remarkable dynamism. International as well as domestic tourism aided by economic factors has become a well-marked feature of the present time. Tourism is a complex dynamic system in the present world, comprised of numerous inter-related and overlapping components or functions. So, tourism can be called as a functional system comprised of five functions or components, tourist attraction, service facilities, transportation and information-direction. However, all the parts are inter-related and influence one-another. The system is dynamic—as one part changes so do all others.

Meaning of Tourism

The meaning of tourism in real terms signifies wider implications. The common man connects tourism with human being who travel his country fill-up with cameras, binocular, maps and guide-books and desirous to enjoy the sights, places such as ancient monuments, temples, stupas, monasteries and lovely mountain panorama. But tourism in the real sense of the term stands more than this. It is an endeavour in which more than these specified human beings are involved. It is more then an endeavour or undertaking. It is an industry composed of many integral parts in which body of organisations of various kinds have a part to play. But tourism is different from other potential export activities simply because the actual consumer of the goods and services gets to the exporting country rather than having most goods and services transferred to him at home. Research and analysis of the economy of tourism, therefore, requires more careful consideration and understanding the true meaning of tourism. Tourism is a complex, dynamic system, comprised of numerous inter-related and overlapping components or functions.

The word 'Tourism' is the transcript of the French word 'Tourism'. That is a very old word. The word 'Tourism' originated in the Nineteenth century. The word 'Tourism' was produced and became popular in 1939's. At that time, it was not so popular and not welcome to the people in the beginning. To-day, the word 'Tourism' has a wider meaning and significance. To-day the word 'Tourist' does not effect the people's mentality psychologically. The spelling means firstly the specialist—for example artist is a person specifying in fine arts. Apart from the vocational sense, alpinist is the translation of mountain climber or lover. The alpinist ventures mountain climbing for indulgence with the body and spirit. As such '1st' has the meaning of specialist in every field concerned. So that we are liable to think the consciousness of elite. Naturally the word 'Tourist' provides the people the meaning of the specialist who enjoy touring.

The word 'Tourism' has been given several meaning. In general, Webster's New International Dictionary defines 'Tourism' as such "Travelling is recreation" and this means other things comprise—activities of the humans beings. So tourist is one who makes a 'tour' or a sight-seeing traveller. Here 'tour' signifies a round or a prolonged journey from place to place for recreation or pleasure. In this sense, the activities of tourists and those who cater for them, can be understood by the word 'Tourism'. The travel may be regarded as touristic if it is made with three essential conditions. These are—(1) travel must be temporary, (2) voluntary and (3) not have remunerated employment as its aim.

Rationally, Tourism does not always have the same meaning and the same scope. If a person can make a journey temporarily, voluntarily and without any remunerated aim within the border of the country (without crossing its frontiers) or beyond the country (outside the country of residence), it is known as Domestic Tourism. The Second example covers the movement of the person not within the country of his residence but outside the country of his residence which means one or many foreign countries, it is termed as International Tourism. To be brief and precise, in case the tourist goes beyond the border of his country, it becomes International Tourism, and in case the tourist goes within the border of his country, it is termed as Domestic Tourism. But this classification does not provide significant meaning just because in Europe—EEC or OECD plays a role to overshadow the significance of border line.

Tourism is the supplying of services to tourists. A tourist exemplifies a person who travels away from his residence, either within his country or abroad and stays away for atleast 24 hours or one night. The reasons for such travel include leisure (recreation, holiday, health, education, religion and sport), business and family matters. A holiday maker, a conference delegate and a travelling business person are all tourists.

Tourism is every activity of mankind for the creation of tourist movement. So the main object of tourism is the movement. If a person goes out of the daily living zone to satisfy his curiosity and his wish to know, to relax, rest and recover his strength in environment different from his usual place of residence for recreation, it is tourism. The persons go out in the outskirts of their own country for recreation. Researchers go out in foreign countries for elaboration of their research works through analyses. In a more elaborate and comprehensive term, tourist is a person who moves to learn, appreciate nature, to relax and for a change in and outside his country.

Definition of Tourism

To define tourism is not an easy task. Casually going through the dictionary, tourism connotes four ways, meaning : *(i)* "the practice of travelling for recreation, *(ii)* "pleasure, or culture", "the guidance or management of tourists", "the promotion or encouragement of touring" and *(iii)* "the accommodation of tourists."

The above definition of Tourism speaks of multiplicity of functions causing the complex of activities, environmental settings and user groups *etc.* in order to understand the real meaning of travel. In a political sense world tourism may be seen to increase international harmony by putting together people of different countries, thus cementing a better appreciation of other life-styles and cultural background. Specially the most important significance of tourism lies in its economic implications.

While defining tourism it is not out of place to mention an Austrian economist Herman Von Schullard who defined tourism for the first time in 1910 as : "The sum total of operations mainly of economic nature which directly relate to the entry, stay and movement of foreigners inside and outside a certain country, city or region."

So tourism is every activity of mankind for the development of tourist movement. In this way, tourism means change, a temporary change in one's way of living, an escapade—even with all its glamour and advantages. Tourism is a right won for all times to come, an integral part of the life of more and more people, and unchangeable trend everywhere.

The fact that many definitions of international tourist exist which are causing a lot of difficulties since different countries of the globe use sometimes one, sometimes the other, when establishing their travel statistics. The definition of the League of Nations which excludes transit travellers or that of the United Nations which as for all other temporary visitors includes them, is used in the case of certain countries which are simply crossed without stopping by a great number of travellers.

Botheration results especially the difficulty of comparing statistics which have to be consulted. To remedy such state of affairs International Union of Official Travel Organisations (IUOTO) took the initiative of proposing a uniform definition. This proposal was discussed at the United Nations Conference on International Travel and Tourism in Rome in 1963.

The text adopted was submitted to the U.N. Statistical Commission which accepted it in 1968 having remarked with certain slight alterations.

The definition uses the general term 'Visitor' as describing any person coming to a country other than of his usual place of residence, for any reason other than to exercise a remunerated profession.

The definition covers two categories of visitors : 'Tourists' and 'Excursionists' which are defined as follows :

'Tourists' are temporary visitors staying atleast 24 hours in the country visited and whose motives for travel are :

(*a*) Leisure (pleasure, holidays, health, studies, religion and sports);
(*b*) Business, family, missions, meetings.

'Excursionists' are temporary visitors staying one day in the country visited without spending the night (including cruise passengers).

The International Union of official travel Organisations (IUOTO) definition states that "statistics should not include travellers who do not legally enter the country", as for example, air travellers who do not leave an airport's transit area or similar cases.

When the member states of the United Nations and all international organisations concerned accept this definition less confusion will reign than does at present.

Then, there will be only two definitions of International Tourism = that of IUOTO for statistical purposes and that of the New York Convention concerning customs facilities for touring.

The economic criterion, however, required that all persons coming to a country to settle or to earn money there, would have to be excluded from the definition. At the same time, the definition precisely defined those not to be considered as tourists were :

— Persons arriving with or without a working contract, to take up an occupation or engage in any business activity in the country.
— Persons coming to establish a residence in the country.
— Residents in a frontier zone and persons domiciled in one country, working in an adjoining country.
— Pupils, students and young persons in boarding establishments and schools.
— Travellers passing through a country without stopping even if the journey takes more than 24 hours.

The omission from the definition of pupils and students in hostel or boarding schools not being considered right since their upkeep is generally maintained by their home members living abroad. The International Union of Official Travel Organisations (IUOTO) took resolution in 1950 to include the category of young people in the definition of Tourist.

Further, the IUOTO was preoccupied with a special category of persons more and more numerous, who visit a foreign country with a touristic aim, for very short period, not exceeding 24 hours and which were not included in the former definition of tourists. These persons are called 'excursionists' to be considered as such, had to travel 'for pleasure' and further, could not undertake 'any lucarative occupation' in the country visited. In fact, the 'excursionists' were nothing more than one-day tourists. Their direction of day is always very short.

International relations, inter-dependence of nations, trans-national investments and business migration for employment, for cultural and religious purposes *etc.* have made contemporary human being aware to travel more and more, faster and farther away.

Such travelling activity is generally quantified and analysed as 'Tourism'. This phenomenon, particularly modern 'mass tourism' is of an increasing economic and social importance worldwide and has more and more direct influence on the very pattern on life in various regions and countries of the world. It leads to setting up and developing, on a large scale, a variety of ancillary activities such as hotels, catering industries, restaurants, motels, camping sites, together with important infrastructures, not to speak of related activities such as handicrafts.

Tourism is every activity of mankind for the development of tourist movement. So the object is the tourist movement. The definition of 'Tourism' given by the Swiss Prof. Hunziker and Krapf is as follows :

"Tourism is the total relationship and phenomena linked with the stay of foreign persons to a locality on condition that they do not settle there to exercise a major, permanent or temporary activity of a lucarative nature."

This definition does not take notice of domestic Tourism. Sociologically the person whatever his destination, either his own country of residence or outside, can travel or stay in the place other than his own, has a very wide significance and this implication has been excluded in the definition.

Other Definition

Visitor, Tourist and Excursionits of :

'Visitor' 1. —Any person visiting a country other than that in which he has usual place of residence, for not more than one year, and whose main purpose of visit is other than following an occupation remunerated from within the country visited.

2. —Any person visiting a country other than that in which he has his usual place of residence, for any reasons other than following an occupation remunerated from the country visited.

'Tourist' 1.—a visitor making atleast a single overnight stay (or a stay of atleast 24 hours) in the country visited and the purpose of whose journey can be classified under one of the following headings :

(*a*) Leisure, (recreation, holiday, health, studies, religion and sport)
(*b*) Business, family, mission, meeting.

2. "Visitors staying atleast 24 hours, but not more than one year, in the country visited and the purpose of whose trip can be classified under one of the following headings :

(*a*) pleasure, recreation, holiday, sport.

(*b*) Business, visiting friends and relatives, mission, meeting, conference, health, studies and religion.

WTO Definition

Excursionist 1. A temporary visitor not making an overnight stay or staying less than 24 hours in the country visited. An equivalent term for 'Excursionist' is 'Day Visitor' and the category may thus include visitors from cruise ships.

2. *WTO Definition*— Visitors, staying less than 24 hours in the country visited (including Cruise passengers)".

Usual Residence : The country in which a person has resided during the year prior to his arrival in the country of destination or prior to his departure from his country of usual residence.

Foreign Visitor

The Statistical Commission of the United Nations Organisation and the Facilitation Commission of the International Civil Aviation Organisation, not finding it possible to accept the definition of the League of Nations, modified by the IUOTO, prepared their own definition not of 'Tourist' but of 'Foreign Visitor'. These definitions differ essentially from that of the League of Nations in that they establish a maximum time limit of stay in the country visited of six months and three months respectively.

Further, the definition of the UN Statistical Commission included in the category of 'Visitors' persons in transit, who were not included in the other definitions.

Another definition was also in the U.N. Convention concerning Customs Facilities for Tourism concluded in 1954 in New York and at present ratified by more than 70 states.

The convention considered as 'tourist' any person coming to a country for a legitimate reason other than immigration, and who stays atleast 24 hours and at most six months during the same year.

None of these definitions refer to the nationality of the tourist, but to the country of usual residence. It follows that even a national of a country visited will be considered as a tourist if he "usually" lives abroad.

International Tourism :

For the first time, as defined above, the definition of International Tourism was considered in 1937 under the aegis of the Economic Commission of the League of Nations. The main view was focussed to make international travel statistics of all countries of the world comparable. The definition runs as follows :

"The term Tourist shall in principle, be interpreted to mean any person travelling for a period of 24 hours or more in a country other than that in which he usually resides."

In the light of the above definition, the following persons are considered as tourist :

— Persons travelling for pleasure, for domestic reason, health etc.
— Persons travelling to meetings or missions of any kind (scientific, administrative, diplomatic, religious, athletic etc.)
— Persons travelling for business purposes.
— Persons arriving in the course of a sea-cruise even when they stay less than 24 hours.

This definition also specified the persons as non-tourist in the following manner :

— Persons arriving with or without a working contract to take upon occupation or engage in any business activity in the country.
— Persons coming to establish a residence in the country.
— Residents in a frontier zone and persons domiciled in one country working in an adjoining country.
— Pupils, students and young persons in boarding establishments and schools.
— Travellers passing through a country without stopping, even if the journey takes more than 24 hours.

The above definition excludes all persons to become a tourist if he comes to a country to settle or to earn money there. The pupils and students in hostels and boarding establishments cannot be excluded as non-tourist as their upkeep is provided by their families living abroad.

Further, the International Union of Official Travel 'Organisations defines' *Excursionists'* as, "a special category of persons who visit a foreign country with a touristic aim, for very short periods, not more then 24 hours."

To make easiness for aviation facilitation purposes, the Statistical Commission of the United Nations and the Facilitation Commission of the International Civil Aviation Organisation prepared their own definitions, not also of 'tourist' but also of 'Foreign Visitor' and they fixed a maximum time limit of stay of a foreign visitor in the country visited to six months and three months respectively. In such a way, visitors in transit were also included in the definition for the first time. U.N. Convention concerning custom facilities for touring concluded in 1954 in New York and at present ratified by more than 70 states. This convention defined *'Tourist'* as any person coming to a country for a legitimate season other than immigration and who stays at most six months during the same year.

With a view to standardizing the International Tourism Statistics is the basis of one and only definition of tourists was considered essential and the IUOTO took the initiative of proposing a uniform definition. This proposal was discussed at the United Nations conference on International Travel and Tourist in Rome in 1963. The text was adopted and then submitted to the U.N. Statistical Commission which accepted it in 1968 after a few minor alterations were made.

The definition uses the general term of 'visitor' as describing any person visiting a country other than that of his usual place of residence, for any reason other than to exercise a remunerated profession.

covers the categories of "Visitor" 'Tourists' and "Excursionists" which are defined as follows :

'Tourists' are temporary visitors staying atleast 24 hours in the country visited and whose, motives for travel are :

(*a*) Leisure (pleasure, holiday, health, study, religion and sports)

(*b*) Business, family, missions, meetings.

'Excursionists' are temporary visitors staying only one day in the country visited spending the night (including cruise passengers).

This definition objects to include transit passenger as tourists in statistical purposes, because he does not legally enter the country.

Now there are only two definitions of 'Tourist' in International Tourism that of IUOTO statistical purposes and that of the New York Convention concerning customs facilities for Touring. The IUOTO definition was accepted by the member states of the United Nations and all international organisations and there is less confusion at present.

To-day, International Tourism concerns all the continent. It is also transforming into mass tourism. The movement of the International tourist between other continents *i.e.* particularly between America, Asia, Australia as well as between Europe and the countries of Near East and Asia has increased tremendously. Africa also is in the world tourism focus. So the world tourists, leaving aside excursionists are millions. Its economic value is immense. It brings in foreign currency and stabilizes the trade balance. World Tourist receipts are recorded in million dollars.

President of the United States, Jimmy Carter in his opening address to the Universal Federation of Travel Agents Association Congress, held in U.S.A. said.

"Travel is a strong influence in the development of human potential and a vital link in the world communication. By visiting other lands, exchanging ideas and making new friendships, we can help to build goodwill and peaceful intercourse among all peoples".

Importance of Tourism

Tourism today presents an unparalleled challenge to the economies of the developing world. The rewards to be gained both financial and socio-economic are immense.

Tourism is a complex, dynamic system comprised of numerous inter-related and overlapping components or functions.

Tourism can be called as a functional system comprised of five functions or components—tourists, attractions, service-facilities, transportation and information-direction. The supply of tourism runs through the entire system and cannot be separated from demand. These characteristics of tourism require that if is to prosper maximize benefits and minimize costs, it must be co-ordinated. Prosperity in tourism comes through co-operation among the components and thus requires group action. The development of tourism must be a co-operative endeavour.

The importance of tourism lays on large sectors of public life and economy. The contribution of tourism to the economy, exceeds that of other sectors in several countries, to the extent that it appears as one of the essential elements in the trade Balance. Tourism is frequently a rapidly expanding sector, the future importance of which — is impossible to produce.

The economic implications, especially of International Tourism are immense. Each country has to keep account of its trade with the rest of the world, it is necessary that it has information of the movements and expenditure of international tourists. A tourist who spends money he has earned at home on tourism in another country, is in fact, 'importing' tourism and the country being visited is 'exporting' it.

Economic Implications of International Tourism

To-day international tourism concerns all the continents. It is also transforming into mass tourism. Each country of the world has to keep account of its trade with most of the world, so it is essential that it has information on the movements and expeditions of international tourist. A tourist who spends money he has earned at home on tourism in other country, is, in fact 'importing' tourism and the country being visited is 'exporting' it. In other words, it is now termed as "Invisible Export."

The movement of the international tourism between the continents *i.e.* particularly between America, Asia, Australia, as well as between Europe, and the countries of Near East and Asia has increased tremendously. Africa also is in the world tourism focus.

International tourism to-day favoured by the economic factors and stimulated by intense publicity has now become a phenomenon characteristic of modern world, widening of horizons to a change in taste and customs and develop the techniques of trade and industry.

Tourism is the fundamental and most desirable human activity worthy of the commendation and encouragement of all people and all governments. So it is termed as one of the most laudable human activity. Besides generating economic activity, it evolves international goodwill and understanding. Besides developing many industries, tourism creates friendship and expands understanding amongst nations. Tourism is a medium through which we can exchange knowledge and create understanding among the people. A large number of people—millions of men—leave their country each year to spend weeks or days in another or in many countries. International Tourism, bringing as it does, men of different nationalities, traditions and beliefs face to face, teaching them the need to get alongwith each other and eliminating prejudices thus becomes a powerful factor in social advancement and for peaceful relation between nations.

Tourism provides direct knowledge and contact with the great achievement of the human world. So it helps to unravel the basic similarities of human feelings without reference to the country and culture. It gives the oneness of feeling which provides a permanent and a fast colour impression of friendliness and communications.

Modern tourism is an instrument of human education. The role of mass tourism is increasing and so it is becoming a powerful tool of education and of collective and individual culture. It discovers the value of manual labour. It conducts to a greater consciousness of the rich heritage of various civilizations and in assimilating about a better appreciation of the inherent values of different cultures. The educative value in tourism is immense as it fosters a feeling of love, understanding, humanitarianism and goodwill far beyond the reach of the mass media or modern method of education.

As part of the cultural role of tourism, the incentives to

local crafts and industries and artistic skills of the people is increased because of the demand for local products and the revival of the folklore, traditional ceremonies, festivals etc. because the tourists are interested in them.

The volume of the tourist receipts depends on an average stay of the tourist in the country. The tourist receiving country endeavours not only to attract the greatest number of international tourist through sophisticated and diversified advertising, but it makes special efforts to create conditions of stay increasingly attractive so that these tourists are tempted to remain as long as possible.

Tourism provides direct employment to millions of people in the hotel industry, transport, travel and trekking business, mountaineering, entertainment, souvenir and also the indirect employment generating out of them.

Tourism is the only export industry that earns large amount of foreign exchange without exploiting national resources and without exporting any manufactured or raw material for development specially for the developing countries for balancing the adverse balance of trade. It helps to lessen the pressure of foreign aid and stimulates for the self-relient development.

Tourism is a terrific influence for peace and improved international contact. It would be affected on the basis of peace, it partakes a part of national diplomacy and provides the people of sense of oneness. The countries are made of individuals and if more and more people of various countries are to visit one another, it would indeed be enviable that social and cultural prevail understanding ?

Domestic Tourism

Apart from International Tourism, Domestic tourism or tourism by residents of a country in their own country, is an important part of tourism. Domestic tourism plays a decisive role in world tourism.

The Manila Declaration's recognition of the real capability of domestic tourism to play a social and educational role to facilitate "opportunity for the citizen to get to know his own environment, a deeper awareness of his national identity and of the solidarity that links him to his compatriots and the sense of belonging to a culture and to a people.[1]

Domestic Tourism has its own substance which provides its motivation and justification. Perhaps part of the substance and the fact that in some cases it requires lower promotion and development costs have made it the most part of world tourism in both industrialized and developing countries.

Definition : "Any person visiting a place other than his normal domicile within the country of his residence, for any activity not remunerated at the place visited (*i.e.* for holiday, business *etc.*), and who makes atleast an overnight (or a 24 hour) stay, may be regarded as a domestic tourist."

In less than a century, domestic Tourism has become a social need. Domestic (internal) Tourism first took mass character. From the close of 19th century, many people, first in Europe, adopted the habit of visiting (on foot, bicycle, train etc.) their own country. They sought to know the treasures and folklore of its different regions and get a taste for travel.

Swiss schoolmaster Topfer in his 'Voyages en Zig Zag' was one of the first of these pioneers. After this, Tourism Associations took prominent part everywhere from 1857 and the British Touring Club—the first of its kind—was also established to promote tourism. At present, Domestic Tourism has become a social phenomenon. It has become a social need everywhere in developed countries.

At present in Europe and America and also in other continents during the holidays and at weekends people travel to the seaside, the mountains or simply the country and visit the cities and regions unfamiliar to them. Domestic tourism statistics though extremely difficult to establish and necessarily incomplete, since it is impossible to know the exact number of those who spend their time with their parents and friends or who stay in tents, show however, the importance of the movement.

Domestic tourism has its own substance which provides

---

1. WTO : Manila Declaration on world Tourism, Document A, Article 8.

its motivation and justification. Perhaps part of this substance and the fact that in some cases it requires low promotion and development costs, have made it the most important part of the world tourism in both industrialized and developing countries.

Domestic Tourism represents a most important but invisible part of total Tourism activity, only a very small part is noticed above the exterior. But domestic tourism activity is obviously a very large part of national economy of any country. It is only now (at present) that is begin to understand it to study it, to research it and to try to put stress on its importance. Over the years, domestic tourism has enjoyed varying degrees of recognition. It is clear that it is becoming more and more important to almost every country.

It is good for all countries not to differentiate between International Tourism Development and promotion from Domestic Tourism Development and promotion. Domestic Tourism represents up to three-quarters of all travel and the plant and facilities are in most cases the response to the needs of national Tourism and only a sort of minor degree, at the periphery are they every made unique for International Tourism.

Domestic tourism is progressively gaining importance in international forum on tourism policy in the present world. Intensified efforts in the area of publicity to promote domestic tourism are presently underway. There is a general trend towards vacations within one's own country. It is becoming more and more important to almost every country. From the development point of view, it is important that it has economic value, that it supports a tourists industry and contributes to employment, capitalization of national economic resources, stimulation of national entrepreneurship, contributs to government tax revenue, assists in the growth of gross domestic product; improvement of lodging and transport infrastructures, influences other interacting sectors of the economy and creation of balance in the population.

The principal socio-economic aim is to fully universalize tourist trips and to make use of tourism as a means of achieving promotion of national economic integration through opportunities it offers, leading to a wider and more equitable distribution of income and most important of all, in its influence on the preservation of the culture and national heritage of the country.

Among the various ways in which leisure is spent, domestic tourism is finding an increasingly important place. The reason of this is, above all that young people of school-going age to-day have a growing desire to see cultural and natural attractions with their own eyes and witness cultural events for themselves.

Domestic Tourism should be a school of democracy for the school children. It breaks down the barriers between different political, social, cultural and ideological groups and enables the young children to mix constantly, thus accustoming them to dialogue, teaching them to respect others and giving them a sense of the common destiny of humanity.

2

DEVELOPMENT OF MODERN TOURISM

Man became restful and stable 5000 years ago when he settled in places where he could till the land. He began to discover implements and tools for working. In such a way, he discovered the wheel at the dawn of civilisation. All this to change to the nomadic wares from one place to another into trips induced by a predetermined purpose but now returning to the place of origin. Some people in the group stayed behind and here new members were born. While going through the outline for travel, at the dawn of civilisation tourism was born. Tourism, as we all know, in fact, signifies a round trip, that is a return trip.

Since ancient times, many accounts of fearless and brave people who went on trips or travels bearing hardships not noticing for limits of human endurance are recorded in the pages of ancient history. There are many accounts of the existence of 'peregrini' which can be noted since ancient times, a pilgrim or traveller in a foreign land—a journey abroad who left on places of religious importance without any fear and anxiety. These intrepid people journeyed braving many dangers, ready to face the troubles which sometimes surpassed the limits for human endurance. The people travelled for interest, curiosity or religious sentiments in ancient times. Three principle motives impelled the ancient people to travel—interest, curiosity or religious sentiments.

Political or Commercial interest

The tribes or states generally took the way to travel for political or commercial interest. The travel of 'envoys' between states or neighbours and also between states, situated at a long distance apart, required the travel for the necessity for Co-existence and good relations. The Rome and China had good Co-existent relations.

After political interest the attraction of great gain on the commercial level, impelled the merchants to take up distant journeys to procure rare and sought after products meeting the fabulous needs of times. The expedition of the Argonauts who sailed in the ship 'Argo' in search of the "Golden Fleece" on way to the orient. Golden fleece—in Greek mythology, is the fleece of the ram Chrysomallus, the recovery of which was the object of the famous expedition of the Argonauts—it gave its name to a celebrated order of knighthood in Austria and Spain founded in 1429.

However, in historical times, the Greeks established colonies along the shores of the Black sea as far as Masseglis (now Marseilles) where their merchants traded with the surrounding people. The Phoenicians created not only the powerful Carthage but traded with the western coasts of Africa. The Arabs travelled as far as China from where they brought back luxury products to their parts of the world. They brought them to Egypt and Italy by the canal which then, like the Suez canal, joined the Red Sea and the Mediterranean. The merchants of Rome toured the shores of the Baltic in search of amber, steel along the length of the Vistula and tin in the British Isles. Such trade exchanges were made in all directions. The merchants approached the well-known coasts in boats, the caravans followed the long trails across the continents.

Curiosity—Generally curiosity impelled people to know the customs, the habits of other peoples, to make long journeys. The Greek historian Herodotus—travelled extensively—travelling many places in Egypt, Mesopotamia, Palestine, Southern Russia and northern parts of Africa. The Romans travelled their own country extensively. The tales of these first 'tourists' of yesteryear (of which Herodotus is the most celebrated) are sometimes the only proof that reminds us of the existence of great civilisations and States, now disappeared, proved more and more by archaeological discoveries.

Religion Sentiments—Religious sentiments persuaded people

to make long pilgrimages to places of venerated worship. The Chinese, followers of Buddha, did not hesitate to go as far as India, travelling thousands of miles, passing desert countries not caring for hardships.

The Greeks and the Romans (known as the Barbarians) went in great numbers to Delphi to hear the Oracle predict the future.

The Greeks organised the Olympic Games for 1,200 years (from 776 BC to 393 AD) and attracted not only the people of Hellas but also the people of all the Roman Empire and even far off countries.

Greeks and Romans also visited the well-known places of curative virtues of certain waters in different spots.

Rome had organised a system of state coach services and security and comfort were also established properly. So the well-to-do people wished to travel to all parts of the Roman Empire to enjoy the natural beauty and many paid visit for amusing themselves at Rome.

By going through these historical accounts of tourism in ancient times, the Romans devised many characteristics of modern tourism. The Romans had also developed seaside resorts and the items of souvenirs. Romans, especially rich people, travelled to Egypt and Greece for making visit to temples and to observe local culture. It is also recorded that the world's first tourist guide book was produced by the Greek geographer Pausanieas for Roman visitors to Greece.

In such a way tourism flourished in ancient times among the people of different states.

The Middle Ages

The fall of the western Roman Empire created havoc and confusion and chaos prevailed everywhere, and so was not very good for making journey due to the insecurity of the route.

Side by side with these happenings, the invasions of the Arabs, the Normans and the Hungarians caused chaos, even then the movement of travelling persons not ceased. Many representatives such as the representative of Charlemagne to

Caliph Haroon-al-Rashid in 797AD or the mission of the two Franciseans of Plano Carmeno and Benedict the Pole sent by the Pope in 1246AD to the far and mysterious Mongolia, are some of the examples.

Trade and pilgrimage were the principal reasons for travel in the middle ages. Merchants journeyed with their goods or popular products liked by the people in big quantity to different destinations. Traders of all nationalities in large numbers participated in the great fairs of St. Denis, Champagne, Aix-la-Chapelle etc. The gathering was Byzantium for the Latin merchants, the Arabs, the Armenians, the Bulgarians, the Chaldeans, the Egyptians, the Persians and the Russians. The merchants undertook sea routes along the European shores of the Baltic, by the Red Sea, and the Atlantic as far as the Mediterranean and the Persian Gulf, across the Indian ocean to Southern China. They took a course of overland routes from Peking or the depths of Africa to all parts of Europe.

These merchants also formed part of sagacious people as for example, the Venetian. Marco Polo or the Arab, Ibrahim Ben Jacob who compiled many tales and useful informations of the countries they visited for providing accounts of that time to the world.

Pilgrimage was very important in the middle ages with the development of western Christianity. Christians took journey to Cathedral towns and religious centres such as Rome, Canterbury in England and the sites of the Holy Land. Hostels and 'hospices' or inns were constructed and developed along the pilgrimage routes.

Another category were the student groups who constituted traveller in the middle ages who used to visit to learn and to hear the speeches of great masters of famous universities: Bologna, Coimbra, Paris, Rome, Salamanca Cracow or the University of Al-Azhar at Cairo, for the Islamic countries.

Many pilgrims continued to travel to the shrines of Lord Buddha. Mecca became a powerful centre of religious attraction for the Islamic countries from the VIIIth century.

Many common people also travelled to many places of attraction and religious significance due to the protection and religious or civil assistance. In such a way, travel in the middle ages was not the privilege of the rich and prosperous people alone, the common people also began to travel.

Modern Times

The situation started to change in the Sixteenth century. The great geographical discoveries led to a change in commercial currents. The old travelling routes for trade were deserted. These changes caused not only the establishment of power states and colonial empires but also to the fall of former Mediterramean Merchant Republics. The character of trade also moved through different moves and changes. The old wandering merchant was replaced by the wholesaler.

Side by side with such arrangement in commercial management, there happened a big change in the pilgrimage as well. The charitable hospices rendering free and comfortable lodging and shelter through benevolent provisions were replaced by the first inns providing lodging and shelter services to pilgrims against payment.

The Renaissance acknowledged the coming up of a new type of traveller. The *Grand Tour* initiated in which young members of the rich or aristocratic family travelled through Europe to be educated and cultivated. So the Renaissance created a new type of travellers who generally liked to visit the famous and picturesque places for pleasure out of curiosity or to acquire knowledge and relaxation. The famous capitals in Europe and British Isles or in other countries having the show of their courts, the famous towns with their historical attractions and monuments and the reputed cultural centres allured visitors from various countries. Renaissance is defined in the Oxford English Dictionary as "The revival of art and letters under the influence of classical models, which began in Italy in the 14th century."

The Industrial Revolution (1760-1840) caused all great technological developments and also effected related changes in all fields of social life, in politics, art, religion, literature and morals and with the rise of democracy and social reforms such changes took place from about 1760 in Britain—the first country to be industrialised. Generally speaking, this industrial revolution produced the economic and social changes arising out of change from industries with power-driven machinery. Such happenings led to a big change in travel patterns and behaviour. The development of railway and the steamship helped inexpensible and swift and easy travel possible for the new middle and working classes. Massive industrial development also caused the opening of mass tourism resorts in the United Kingdom (U.K). Even then, Tourism and Travel remained very expensive and leisure time was not available to the working classes and those who held salaried positions did not have the right to a paid holiday in the 19th century.

Importance of paid holidays and naturally of leisure time activities resulted in the flow of tourism. Between 1850 and 1960 the reduction in the weekly working hours in industrialised Countries resulted in an increase of 24 hours of lėisure time per week in many professions. It is believed that in the industrialized countries the average man now has 22 years more of free time than his grandfather. Such an increase in leisure time for the masses was due greatly to technical progress which has widen production and increased income with concurrence reduction of working hours. It is realised that the industries have helped their workers in utilizing properly their leisure time and this tendency is still now undergoing constant expansion for the future. There are now many kinds of activities for leisure time such as theatre, cinema, hotels and restaurants, books, newspapers, periodicals, sports events and outdoor recreation. So these factors have most permanently influenced tourism development. The availability of free time is a pre-requisite to deciding to undertake tourist travel. Due to the nature and increasing tendency to have more than one annual period of holidays (summer-winter), the reduction of the work-week and the growth in the number of days of annual leave are determining factors in the development of the tourist demand. Constant reference has now been made to paid holidays as being a prime factor in the development of

Tourism. The Manila Declaration states :

> "Modern tourism results from the adoption of a social policy which led to the workers gaining annual paid holidays and represents the recognition of fundamental rights of the human beings to rest and leisure."[1]

An important date throughout the world was 1936, when many states signed an International Convention undertaking to develop paid holidays *(convention No. 52 on paid holidays—International Labour' Organisation).* After that, leisure activities have become accessible to all and this came about only when governments enacted labour legislation introducing paid holidays in true source of modern tourism. Social Legislation recognises leisure. This has limited the number of working hours and ensured for all workers, employers and labourers, a Weekly Rest and an Annual Paid Holiday. As said above, the International Labour Organisation took the initiative of drawing up convention on Paid Holidays in 1936 and modified it in 1949, fixed this minimum at six week-days per year. Many countries now provide the annual paid holiday for the workers. So the man at present has at his disposal leisure to travel. In such an atmosphere, the development of modern tourism is due to the economic and social factors. These factors led great human masses to an opportunity for travel which was formerly the privilege of small groups of rich people. Now freedom to travel is one of the Rights of man:

On December 10, 1948, the General Assembly of the United Nations adopted and proclaimed, the Universal Declaration of Human Rights, setting out thirty inalienable freedoms for all citizens of the member states of the United Nations.

Article 13 states : (1) "Everyone has the right to freedom of movement and residence within the borders of each state".

(2) "Everyone has the right to leave any country, including his own and to return to his country."

Similarly, Article 24 of the Universal Declaration states:

---

1. WTO: Manila Declaration on World Tourism, Document A, Article 14.

"Everyone has the right to rest and leisure, including reasonable limitation of working hours and periodic holidays with pay."

Here, it is good to move ahead with understanding the meaning of leisure. There are many negative definitions. In 19th century, the idea of leisure was considered as surplus hour excluding labour hours plus necessary hours for daily life *i.e.* meal time, the time for call of nature. The idea was born at the time of starting period of Industrial development.

There are many types of leisure such as

(*a*) Resting leisure—bodily rest without any purpose, loitering,

(*b*) leisure for adjustment—positive adjustment of the body-recreation,

(*c*) leisure for fixed purposes to plan to recreate the value which is unable to get without leisure.

The argument on the system of two holidays a week has appeared fiercely.

So the socio-psychology on the leisure must be considered while going deep on leisure. The existing value of leisure is a place which repairs injuries of humanity by labour but recently mass leisure has been noticed. So even in the leisure, the human may be injured. Mass leisure has been given by the mass communication which agitates co-harmony and so independence of humanity may be getting loss. To avoid the loss of human independence, the people in the present world must plan leisure in the whole life of human being. Recently, many enterprises have directed employees to utilize their leisure time to keep them in good condition. The increase in leisure time is the worldwide trend. The adoption of automation provides the workers less hours to work. So, for the workers 5 days a week is the target. The word "Leisure" is the originally free period between the working hours which does not cover up the meaning of the increase in leisure. In this sense, many thanks to the mass-communication which the present people imported the word 'Vacance' in French, which word is best suitable in the present situation.

Modern Tourism

Modern tourism is an instrument of human education. The role of mass tourism is increasing. It is day by day growing as a more powerful instrument of education and of collective and individual culture. It finds out the value of mankind's labour. It also helps to know more of one's own country and its historic traditions and its cultural values. It widens the knowledge of other peoples habits, their way of life and many other things causing love and affection for humanity. Tourism creates better understanding among peoples, it fosters greater awareness of the rich heritage of various civilisations and in inducing a better appreciation of the innate values of various cultures. So tourism is of indispensable value for human education. Due to the immense value of tourism United Nations Educational Social and Cultural Organisation (UNESCO) has regarded tourism as a basic instrument of education. The United Nations declaring 1967 as International Tourist Year, a formal recognition has been given to the fact that the economic and social impact of tourism is real and of great significance.

Tourism is to-day the largest single item in world trade, fetching in its fold tremendous economic development, side by side, increasing economic growth and prosperity. It also makes amity between different peoples of the world, socially and culturally and fosters to one another's beliefs and mores and tolerance towards other customs. In such a way, it comes to turn to a powerful factor in social achievement and peaceful relations between nations.

Tourism gives a direct knowledge and contact with the great achievements of the human mind. So it helps to unravel the basic similarities of human emotions irrespective of country and culture. This kind of a feeling creates an everlasting impression of friendliness and communication. It is therefore, one of the most laudable human activities. Besides generating economic activity, it evolves international goodwill and understanding. So tourism, while developing many industries, builds friendship and enlarges understanding amongst nations. Tourism is a channel through which we can promote knowledge and understanding among the peoples of the world and build up the prospect of establishing the lasting foundations of a world community.

For importing idea of international understanding and co-operation, the World Tourism Organisation has played an active role in the development and organisation of national and international tourism in general and has been of special assistance to its full and associate members in particular. This organization has been instrumental in invigorating tourism and bringing social and economic values of tourism to the attention of the world leaders and social science researchers. It has been acting as the spokesman of tourism and has been the source of reliable tourism data and statistic. It has, no doubt fostered the most dramatic change in man's understanding of tourism.

The World Tourism Organisation is striving hard to help and assist its more than one hundred member states to consider tourism and its problems in its new dimensions as one of the most significant expressions of modern civilization. It is due to this organisation, that every year September 27 is designated to celebrated as World Tourism Day to arouse consciousness among its member states to strengthen the well-known and well- publicized attribution of tourism. It is because of this consideration that world Tourism Organisation's fundamental role will continue to promote and develop tourism worldwide, with particular emphasis to the developing countries and with a view to contributing to economic progress and fostering international brotherhood and understanding.

Tourism prospers on peace. It can be successful only in an peaceful atmosphere and it would be effective on the condition of peace. It shares views independent of national diplomacy and provides the people of all nations a sense of unification.

Tourism, the extra-ordinary phenomenon of modern society, can be developed only when all the nations of the world desire to progress it as the driving wheel of all economic activities and a source of national wealth alongwith powerful instrument of peaceful co-existence and harmony.

3

KINDS OF TOURISM

We have made it clear in chapter one that international tourism signifies the movement of a person or tourist who goes beyond the border. But in case of Domestic Tourism tourist goes within the borders of his country. Domestic Tourism makes movement of the local currency of one's own country, but International Tourism provides foreign currency.

While going ahead, it is proper to rationalize different views of Tourism. Tourism can be (a) Passive Tourism, and (b) Active Tourism. *Passive Tourism* is not concerned so much for the existence of tourist will as for example leader will command everybody—set tour, package tour etc. But in the case of Active Tourism—tourist has his own will to decide *i.e.* Free Tour. It has gradually increased inclination from Passive Tourism to Active Tourism under the motto—Do it yourself Travel Recreation—only to apart from the daily zone for relaxation.

There are kinds also of *Tourism for Appreciation* which can be sub-divided into type of the relaxation and tour. Tourism for appreciation, such as flower viewing, mountain-viewing, autumn leaves-viewing *etc.* is very original and this type of relaxation is to escape daily routines—mental or physical *i.e.* change of air after recovery from illness. Similarly, tour to go to the temples or shrines, appreciate the scenery, to see the festivals *etc.* are all Tourism for Appreciation.

There are also *Tourism for Action,* which can be sub-divided by types of pleasure-seeking and of physical education. *i.e.* not only to view mountain or rocks but to climb it. Types of pleasure-seeking tourism collecting shells in the beach, rock stone gathering which forms part of Physical Education—the exercise of moving our body. Webster's New International Dictionary defines Tourism 'Travelling is recreation'—other things comprise activities of the human being. In general term, tourism is every activity of the mankind for the development of tourist movement—object is the tourist movement.

Social Tourism implies only elites who afford to travel, but now everybody likes to travel. Tourist movement is classified into two—go and come. In the touristic places, all put their emphasis on the word 'come' to invite, even if the nation is also on the same policy. The subject of tourism is divided by two, for example— *(i)* fostering tourism which is the purpose of public benefit, and *(ii)* Tourist Enterprises—the purpose of earning money. Fostering tourism requires comprehensive publicity of touristic resorts, arrangements of touristic resorts and to improve the quality of guides. Side by side with these improvements, local bodies and judicial person for public welfare are to be utilized alongwith Tourist Enterprises as private person comparing local bodies and even states. Perfect example can be cited as an example: Gambling in Monaco.

Here, it is not out of place to refer just inter-change of Tourism and Tourism itself is the point of history. With the touristic trend, there is a fact of movement in the pursuit of recreation. When the mankind was born, the efficiency for the improvement of tourism has been provided some artificial measures. Hence, origin of Tourism, just after World War I (1914-19) originating in Germany, Italy, Great Britain and then France.

In the Point of Geography—wherever people exist, there is a trend of tourism. Fostering tourism is not worldwide. In advanced countries they are making an effort. While under-developed countries, they do not put their emphasis, because of shortage of finance and facilities.

The effect of tourism in the economic side generally is considered and divided it through the direct tourism. So it means net income as for the hotel construction, other relating enterprises, getting in touch with it, which assist gradually increased employment and relating enterprises.

The effect of amity—Tourism is the peace industry. It would be effected on the basis of peace. It partakes apart of national diplomacy and tourist movement provides the people a sense of unification.

The effect of culture—Tourism is also a developed interchange of cultural tie. The culture has its essence which flows from the high to low for which the development is carried out through means of tourism. As a result of tourism, various facilities have been arranged which help the industries go along with them.

With the above phenomenon of tourism, it is necessary to know about the contents of Tourism. Tourism itself is constituted of two elements such as *firstly*, the inside element of the people—wish for tourism, everlasting consciousness for recreation, and *secondly*, outside element of the people concerned-matter of Tourism. It has served tourism through the means of (1) and (2) having the go-between of tourism. The first clause is sub-divided into consciousness and non-consciousness. In case, there is a feeling of what person likes to move. It is related in the field of psychology of tourism. Lastly, movement itself which concerns with the transportation facilities which are possible to move and the accommodation facilities and even roads walked on them. Then comes the Tourist will which concerns *(i)* Touristic will, and *(ii)* Go-between plus concern makes matters of Tourism. Tourist will can be created by publicity which entrepreneur is to be given some works to other people. The just meaning of 'Go-between' means receipt which signifies welcome. It goes well between the harmony of one and two.

So, Tourism means that one goes out of its daily living zone, planning to get back for recreation for which is to move. Subject is their living zone. The essence is to move and the purpose is recreation. The condition to move aparting from the daily living zone and to get back to the same place. Having the ideas of kinds of Tourism as amplified above, now it is essential to write in detail some types of tourism.

Classification of Tourism

The motives of tourism are varied in the case of

International tourism. The diversity of touristic motivations is accorded or entrusted equal to the diversity of the types of tourism which can be seized in the modern world. It is proved that the regions of the different parts of the world tender an immense variety of attraction. So it is needed firstly to study the types of Tourism which a country has the big potentiality of development in a given time. A person usually makes a varied kind of Travel and even visiting one country can experience certain characteristic types of tourism.

Some very important types of tourism can be classified as follows:

Pleasure Tourism—Pleasure tourism embraces of holiday out of curiosity, to relax, to enjoy new places and sights, view good scenery, unique folklore, the peace and calm of the country or the entertainments provided by big cities and showy modern tourist spots. Some person find pleasure in travelling, from the constantly changing place and surroundings. This type of tourism is associated with the idea of pleasure, changes according to the tastes and the background, character and temperament of each person.

Pleasure motivated activities (for example, beaches and exploration) or education activities (tours of historical monuments), tours of scenic areas of outstanding panorama and natural beauty, national parks and wildlife, sea and mountain resorts; entertainments, participation and viewing sports; amusements and recreation parks, zoos and ocenariums cinema and theatre, night life and crusade which gives pleasure to the senses or pleasurably exhalts the mind and spirit. The harmony or unity of all the parts of a site or landscape observed by a person represents the pleasure tourism.

Cultural Tourism—This type of tourism comprises of holiday out of a variety of motivations, linking of desire to learn and to study in a place famous for its high standard of teaching, to absolve in the study of the habits, the life and the institutions of peoples different from their own, visit to historical monuments of historical importance and past civilizations. So the cultural sites and areas of archaeological interest; historical buildings and monuments; places of historical significance;

museums, modern culture; political and educational institutions, and religion represent cultural tourism. Side by side, with these elements traditions—national festivals, arts and handicrafts items, folklore and native life and customs are also part of cultural tourism. A visit to the famous modern centre of achievement, art galleries, the famous religious centres, to visit or to participate in art festivals and celebrations and to take part or indulge in music, theatre, dance and folklore festivals. The quality of tourism is enhanced by the cultural elements which create unique environment. Dance, music, art and architecture of all varieties communicate the concept through emotion and visual preceptors. These resources stress the communality of human emotion and sensitivity.

Recreational Tourism—This type of tourism is pursued by people who visit places of holidays to rest, reinstate their physical and psychic strength, and to get relief from tedium, disgust and weariness. Generally such type of tourism is of longer duration. People like to remain at the places selected for such holidays, for the longest period of time. People like to stay longer time for relaxation by the sea beach, in the green lovely mountains, in sanitorium for relished comfort. Many climatic resorts now exist in different parts of the world and people like to visit such places for stay and recuperation. In order to maintain their health in good state, some people visit and stay on the SPA or Convalescent Resorts for improving their health conditions.

Tourist experience ranging from the recreational (temporary relief from work-a-day lives through leisure or entertainment) to the essentials, quite different from the tourist's own society and culture. So the recreational travel is of an educational and informatic character since they also exclude sightseeing, climate, health resorts or spas and unique attractions. The visual environment plays a major role in recreational tourism.

Sporting Tourism—Sporting Tourism refers to the elements concerned with the devotees which comprise of winter sports, nautical sports, mountain climbing, horse riding, hunting, fishing, rafting in the swift flowing rivers etc. It is known and noticed that countries having one of these sport facilities in their land, have the good chance to attract many devotees and thus benefit from this type of tourism.

While dealing with this type, it is better firstly to come across its two separate features. The foremost one is the big sports events—like the Olympic Games, the Continental or World cricket, football, boxing, sking and swimming championships *etc.* which allure to the country not only the sportsmen but also large number of followers and sport-interested people. This type of Tourism provides recreation, pastime, dalliance, amorous behaviour, play, a game full of mirth played by skilled sportsman which gives a good spirit for sports fans or their followers. Sporting events cause an exhilerating and amusing merriment to the sport followers for viewing sportsmanship relating with every kind of games.

Business or Technical Tourism—This type of tourism deals with one engaged in commercial transactions. Business refers to trade, profession or occupation and so it is related with commercial activity or industrial concern. Though controversial opinions expressed by many theoreticians, including sociologists as well as economists, referring this type of tourism goes outside the 'Voluntary' element of a tourist travel. The term 'Business Tourism' refers not only the professional journeys of businessmen or industrialists but also all journeys which have their aim of visit to fairs and exhibitions, or of technical achievements, or of technical techniques which infuse a new knowledge and interest among people concerning their profession. While visiting for their business tour, the businessman can be real tourists by making their visits to places of interests, for sightseeing of natural or cultural attractions during their visit in order to enjoy the recreation and relaxation provided by the visiting country. Many countries now are interested in developing such type of tourism by strengthening business and technical contacts.

Convention or Conference Tourism—This type of tourism is gaining great popularity in the present world. With the scientific and technical revolution, the nations of the world wish to develop close relations and exchange experiences in developing material and cultural values which is reflected in strengthening professional and scientific contacts. This phenomenon has led to new type of international tourist ties, Convention or Conference Tourism. Many conferences, International Congresses, assemblies, symposia are held every, year all over the country.

These conferences and meetings are of immense importance as these attract many or in some thousands of participants. These delegates make their duration of stay longer in the city or the country hosting such events. It goes without saying that delegates to a convention or Congress are also tourists since, they go for sightseeing during the convention or the Congress and often take post-convention tours. Now certain cities are famous for hosting conferences in the best possible ways and are organising regular conventions, conferences and meetings. Such countries are organising conferences and are best prepared to receive the delegates. Such country also organises many international exhibitions which draw people from all over the world. Many tourist resorts are gaining popular as conference towns and are popular for this purpose (Belgium, France *etc.*).

Many tourist come to the country in special professional groups with the express purpose of meeting their counterparts and exchanging experiences. Some country or professional associations of variety of trade prepare special programs for these groups including visits to enterprises and establishments that reflect the professional interest of the group.

So convention tourists (a form of business tourist) are the travellers moving worldwide for the purpose of conventions/conferences/meetings or special events. The major convention organizing cities in Europe are France, Geneva, London, Brussels, Vienna, Barcelona and Straberg, while such major cities in Asia are Manila, Tokyo, Singapore, Hong Kong and Seoul. Many countries realize the importance of this type of Tourism, endeavour to prepare suitable premises or even to construct 'Conference halls' with all modern equipments to ensure their satisfactory operation. These conventions organizing cities are making good economic gains from such organisations, since convention tourists are the affluent class tourists.

Resort Tourism—This type of Tourism consists largely of tourists seeking sun and sand, staying in generally large hotels and often travelling but not always on a group tour that includes transport, room and board in one package. Resort tourism has been particularly important in developing countries that have secured rapid and large-scale growth in the number of tourists from Europe and North America. Such type of Tourism consists for the quest for sun, sand and sea or rum or rooms and recreation which are full of facilities and excessive costs. Most of the social life in such a type of tourism revolved around the luxury hotels and casinos. The hotels in such resorts provide first class restaurants, ball-rooms, game rooms, gardens and sport facilities. Most of such establishments are located on sheltered hills where tourists can enjoy the visual mix of sun and breezes and where they can maintain their separation from the local populace. Many mountain spas or resorts offer a wide variety of entertainment. The first Riviera Resort to profit from games of chance was the Principality of Monaco since French towns were prohibited from opening casinos until 1884. After this date, a new type of tourist—the gambler began to predominate on the Mediterranean coast.

Pilgrimage Tourism—The term Pilgrimage tourism commonly presumes a focus on performing travel to religious places of importance. Religious pilgrimages, tourism situations that are of overwhelming importance in certain places such as Mecca, 'Lourdes' and of secondary relevance elsewhere in such places as Jerusalem, Rome etc. Pilgrims create special demands and possibilities. In such type of Tourism, religious ceremonies, cultural manifestation that directly involve the people, their culture and their way of life. Temple services and religious ceremonies for the artistic performances derived from the religious texts depicting the story and epic representation and in general for the appealing life-style of the people. A rich inheritance of religious artifacts which embrace not only historic houses, castles, temples, stupas *etc.* but also stretch from pre-history (standing stones relics or brochs). A clearly defined religious identity is expressed in religious performances, music, customs, language and architectures. Tourists from abroad can enjoy and religious renowned ensembles as they travel through the religious places of the country.

Formations of Tourism

Having known the aspects of tourism, it is now easy to understand the forms or formation of tourism and its duration or economic effects. International and Domestic tourism, both can be divided into individual Tourism and organised or collective tourism. Individual Tourism means a person or a group of persons make by themselves a tour itinery and a destination and go for a tour and such travel can be changed at any time in accordance with the wishes of the organiser. Organised tour, on the other hand, signifies a tour or journey organised by a travel agency to any person or group of persons interested against payment of an all-inclusive amount following a programme and time-table made in advance. In such a tour the person or group of persons do not bother about the provisions and services which are well- organised and assured by the organiser.

A Tourist industry, is composed of all the activities that directly supply goods and services for the tourists. The industry comprises international and domestic airlines, shipping companies, ferry operations, railway, bus and taxi operations, accommodations, restaurants, clubs and other catering establishments, tour and excursion operations, travel agents, promoters of entertainment facilities, national parks managements, souvenir suppliers, tourist information centres, conference, convention and meeting centres. These facilities and services serve nationals (non-tourists) as well.

Forms of Tourism based on the length of the journey can be called Long-term Tourism and Short-term Tourism, making of Weekend or Excursion. Long-term Tourism means a journey of long stay for several weeks or months, Short-term Tourism signifies a journey of a week or ten days. This form of tourism is useful for a clientale unable to go on long holidays.

Excursion Tourism is defined as a journey not exceeding 24 hours and without accommodation having to be provided. Such form of tourism is favourable in the border areas where the right kind of exchange provides worthy purchase to be tranjected at the time of a journey.

There is also the different forms of tourism according to the means of transport used, such as rail, cruises, air, road and motorised tourism. Pedestrian tourism—trekkers or hikers are also distinguished as another form of tourism.

Tourism by its economic effects can be distinguished as Receptive Tourism in the case of International Tourism which brings foreign tourist arrivals with foreign currency into a country causing its effects on the balance of payments. If the resident of a country goes abroad with foreign currency, is called Passive Tourism as it has a negative effect on the balance of payments.

Then, there are two forms of Tourism—Domestic (National Tourism) and International Tourism. It is apparent that the person if he goes within the border of his country it becomes Domestic Tourism and if he goes outside the border of his country, it becomes International Tourism. But the main object of tourism in both cases is the same when the person makes his movement within or outside the country of his residence for the object of the touristic interest to any area or objects. In economic aspect only, there lies some difference as in case of International Tourism it brings foreign currency but Domestic Tourism only makes movement of the local currency.

Lastly, going through the forms of tourism it is almost relevent that the motivation and the aims for travel can be observed especially on the form in which the journey is carried out on its duration or its economic effects.

4

TOURISM RESOURCES

Tourist Supply And Historical Resources

Tourism is a complex, dynamic system, embraced of many inter-related and wrapping components or functions. Therefore, tourism can be termed of five functions or components and information-precept. Each of these part is complex and can again be separated into various divisions. But even then, all the parts are inter-related and induced one another. The nature of the components overlap and can be one thing at one time and another thing at another time. Facilities, services, transportation, information can be attractions and vice-versa. The supply of tourism passes through the whole system and cannot be turned away from demand. These characteristics of tourism need that if it is to develop—maximize benefits and minimize costs by co-ordinating all aspects connected with it. Prosperity in tourism comes through co-operation among the components and stands in need to groups action. The type and extent of group action may differ but rarely will government be left out.

Tourism is pervasive. Whenever, tourism exists and there are few places unaffected it becomes an integral part of the social and economic fabric. Tourism affects the lives of everyone, either as tourists or as recipients. Tourism competes for resources and in such case it may be agreeable to some activities of an area, it may clash with states of the lifestyle and create costly impacts. Success of these impacts may be the responsibility of government. So the decadence of falling of tourism is one of the strongest argument for government involvement.

Motivations for tourism differ. In the case of tourist entrepreneurs while profit or return on investment is particularly the single most prime motive, however, is not always the case. Few entrepreneurs want to lose money as a fair show but some may desire to maximize other benefits such as goodwill or a desired lifestyle. But tourism may be a way to improve relations with other nations of the world, increase or earn foreign currency, reduce social unrest by providing jobs or maintaining economic productivity by supplying leisure opportunity and rest.

Strategies for the development of tourism supply or developing tourism strategy must be a co-operative endeavour. It requires in one form or another groups action. It may dispense international co-operation between, among and within different agencies and levels of government; co-operation between government and businesses and relations between, among and within different types of businessess. Co-operation may be formal or informal, but some mechanism for expediting co-operation are necessary. While businesses within one sector of tourism may function co-operatively through associations, in the final analysis, government may be required to play the key role in overall co-operation in tourism.

The role of the government is very important and engage or be a proponent of tourism planning. While it may carry out all the functions of planning, it may serve only as a catalyst for planning. Positively, planning forms in identifying problems and opportunities, setting goals and objectives and developing strategies to accomplish the goals. Substantial to the process are facts and data, synthesizing of these facts and data, creativity and conceptualization, feedback and modification and decision making.

Facts and data on the nature and dimensions of tourism supply are critical to the planning process. We all know that government generally plays a leadership role in the entire planning process, collecting the facts and data of tourism supply. Whether or not such information is used for planning, it is the basic ingredient out of which marketing, advertising, promotion and information programs are made.

Only when goals and objectives are stated does it begin to become clear what kinds of data are required. Even though they may be poorly defined, every action performed by government, businesses or individual is forecasted upon goals and objectives. Generally, the goals of tourism have been perceived to be increased economic activity or profit objectives are defined to help reach the goals. Thus, any action taken in tourism must be carried out in the context of goals and objectives. Generally, National or State Tourism Administration policy is founded upon a set of fairly broad goals.

So tourism has importance in a country's economy. Tourism involves the pursuit of economic industry. Touristic resources may be called touristic supply in general and they mean the objective and deed to potentials. Tourism economy will be changeable with the balance of supply and demand. Therefore, touristic consumption refers to more continuously for the potentials. In the touristic goods, they have different points from ordinary goods due to their unbarterable character.

In order to know the tourist supply, we must know the market. Supply is one of the two elements of market. In economic standings and in the broad sense that market is the theoretical point of convergence of supply and demand. The market is the embodiment of transactions of sale and of purchase and manifests the adjustment between production and consumption. The total of transactions in liberal economy influences prices. The market always includes two essential elements—a supply and a demand; in the non-existence of one of them, the market does not exist. The services market differs considerably from a consumer goods market . A service market has got some specific characteristics as compared to consumer goods market which is as follows :

- It concerns with human labour which cannot be replaced by technical means as for example housework, bar tender, guides and interpreters.
- The product for tourism cannot be stocked because the service must be provided at the needed hour and time, not before nor after.

— The consumer must be served at a given moment.
— The demand for personal services is more irregular.
— The supply of services always has a certain degree of elasticity.

The outline of tourism as described above makes clear that will + Leisure + Shopping cause demand. So the facilities, potentials equal supply.

Touristic Resources may be called the Touristic supply in general but generally it means the objective and deed to potencils. It is a proved fact that Tourism economy will be changeable with the balance of supply and demand.

Touristic consumption means to more continuously for the potentials. In the touristic goods, they have different points from ordinary goods, *i.e.* unbartable goods.

Tourist goods will cost Fine price because they have additional value—original Cost + Alpha.

Touristic consumption (1) Traffic Payment (2), Payment for boarding and lodging, and (3) Payment for appreciation.

The factors of touristic demand depend on the following elements : (1) The strength and weakness of shopping; (2) Change of season, and (3) Change of local economy.

Tourist industry effects intensely the local economy. Tourist industry will be effective to national economy as for example domestic (internal and external factors), internally to effect the levelness of wage. Externally, foreign visitors will bring in foreign currency.

Tourist supply is very particular and at the same time contains peculiarities. The tourist resources are localized and fixed. So the tourist services cannot be stocked. While making clear of the topics made above, it is better to illustrate by example, such as mountain climbing is possible by visiting the place where there are high mountains. The tourist or say mountain climber must visit by himself the place of having high mountains to enjoy mountain climbing. The consumption of tourist service is made possible by travel which means a person must make a journey from his country to the tourist resource.

The 'Tourist Service' is a combination of Economic

(measurable) and Non-Economic (immeasurable) goods. Tourism can be expressed by tickets purchased for motor car, railway, air etc. which can be consumed and measured at the same time, the pleasure of the eyes—visiting historical sites, natural panorama, relaxation and recreation which cannot be measured.

Tourist services are highly specialised as accommodation, transport, recreation etc. The tourist himself must come to various 'specialised markets' for the satisfaction of his needs.

Tourist supply has a relatively low degree of elasticity, as most tourist plant concerns only a single need. The tourist plant is specifically made for the use of tourists only and not for others. A residential hotel cannot be a tourist hotel because of its simple facilities. Ski-lifts, pleasure boats, luxury coach for sight-seeing, *etc.* have their own specialities and they are made to serve the tourists with the first-class service arrangements and decor.

The tourist market is dynamic as it envelopes wide range of goods and services to an ever-increasing clientete.

The efforts to increase the tourist income depends upon the following factors :

(1) tourism is something of a movement, so it is necessary to have or to promote good traffic system,

(2) it is also necessary to improve the rate of currency for the tourist, and

(3) to check and control the problem of the prices between the tourist regions. Specially, not to use tax for the tourist as for as possible.

So the idea of touristic economy makes it clear that we should not be far from the ideal of touristic economy, so we have to grasp the ideal clearly and access it with all analysis.

Richness of touristic resources must be maintained to attract international tourists. The occurrence of tourists is necessary because tourism is now one of the life target in the consumption. The distribution of tourists, firstly, the distribution at present at the places of attractions, should be researched and in a certain touristic site from external arrival should be researched.

The tourist economy can be maintained properly if the richness of touristic resources (*a*) to conserve nature, (*b*) conservation of culture, (*c*) to make good use of resources by promotion of touristic supply; (*d*) establishment of facilities in high quality submission, and *(e)* to acquire the demand to the limit of supply.

The Tourism and Travel Industry including developers, travel agencies, hotels and so forth, have an opportunity and responsibility to help maintain the healthy environment on which their business relies. Governments cannot be expected to carry the entire burden themselves, so the tourism industry as a whole, should do everything in its power to encourage more effective conservation action. Tourism nature as well as culture are natural partners and each can benefit from one another if all are properly managed. Sufficient resources must be developed to managing the natural and cultural areas in order to have the development of tourism properly as well as effectively.

THE TOURIST HERITAGE

The concept of heritage is quietly modern as it rises from man's awareness of the finite quantity of the Earth's resources and the oneness of human society. It imports the collective responsibility of mankind for the conservation of natural, built and social-cultural resources.

Going through the dictionary definitions of the culture, they have not properly defined it and so have done injustice to the heritage concept.

In the plain manner, the tourist heritage can be defined as follows :

"The touristic heritage (of a country, a region, or a locality) is the combination of elements likely to attract the attention of Tourists and provoke a visit by them. This combination represents the supply of the tourist market. It may have its source in a spa, a monument, a ski-slope, or a well-known hotel or restaurant.

"Tourism derives its existence not only from the gifts provided by nature but also from elements created by the activity of Man."[1]

Webster Dictionary defines heritage as : "Something transmitted by or acquired from a predecessor."

The notion coming short of in the above definition of Webster is that of responsibility. The present generations have their responsibility to hand over to future generations, the assets they have inherited. The possession or importance of heritage must not be worth handing over to future generations, it must be added, enhanced and restored by the coming generations.

The natural values are very important elements of tourist heritage. These values are varied and the following features which help visitor's attractions can be referred :

1. The valleys and dales of countryside which consist of interesting forms, unusual formation panorama, colour of land, rocks, gorges etc.
2. The mountain and its sites : (alpinism)
3. The climate : temperature, atmosphere precipitation, rain and snow, days of sunshine, etc.
4. The Verdant Contents : thick forests, types, rare and unusual trees.
5. Water body : water course, springs, lakes, ponds, big rivers, waterfalls, etc.
6. The Wild Flora and Fauna : wildlife of all kinds, the arrangement of hunting and fishing, uncommon vegetation, National parks, reserves, conservation areas, protected species, zoos, etc.

Here it is necessary to realize that a single component of native exceptionally attracts the interest of tourists. In reality, a blending of various elements which make up the natural environment or setting probability to sustain and maintain tourist inflow.

Side by side with natural values which cause the form of the great types of tourist region. The important types of natural touristic regions are :

---

1. *Source* : International Union of Official Travel Organisations, Correspondence Course from Tourism Studies—Geneva, 1971.

— Costal Areas
— The Mountains.

Visitors visit mountain in summer for picturesque sights and climate or in winter for skiing or mountaineering.

The country and forests are also becoming at present more and more attractive and visitors like to see deserts and oases; tropical stolks and small islands, tolders, marshes and boating areas, volcanic areas, just for experience.

There are values created by the activity of man which are also part and parcel of touristic heritage. Among these, should be mentioned particularly :

— Historical Monuments : palaces, castles, forts, monasteries, religious edifices and other architectures etc.
— The important places of History and Civilisation—their ruins, archaeological excavations, art galleries, museums, archives, libraries, memorials, monuments, folklore etc.
— Popular Art : Rural houses, handicrafts production, folklore, etc.
— Traditional Events : Popular religious and civil festivals and events, popular pilgrimages, exhibitions, sports, meetings etc.
— Industrial or Technical Tourism—Scientific stations (Atom), big dams, factories processing original or regional products (sugar mines, plantations, dairies etc.)
— Spa Installations—Spas have played an historical role since earliest time. Hot springs, and other places having the curative values of mineral waters to make either therapeutic or a prophylectic care have played large number of visitors since earliest times.

Tourist Heritage Must be Protected

The tourist heritage is the series of elements likely to attract the attention of international visitors and stimulate a sojourn by them. Thus combination represents the supply of the tourist market. It has its source in a countryside, mountain temples, stupas, a monument, the climate, the salvan element, springs, lakes, waterfalls, and the wild flora and fauna.

Nature contributes the greatest source of wealth of the tourist heritage. The natural values are generally varied and so making tourist development there must be proper thinking and management to upkeep the harmonious balance of biological phenomena. The natural phenomena of the country must be preserved at any cost and every care should be taken not to destroy and damage the natural beauty. Many countries have now realised the value of natural surroundings and they have developed series of legislative provisions to protect natural environment and to check the waste of nature. International organisations are also keen to foster the attention of the world and to educate and develop consciousness on the natural environment and its value for mankind. Now many nations of the world have created many National Parks, Reserves, Conservation areas in their country to protect nature in their pristine glory. Pollution has now increased very much in the name of modern development due to population growth, urbanisation, the establishment of factories or industries for production, deforestation, use of pesticides, use of automobiles such as car, buses, airplanes, railways *etc*. The waste of natural elements due to overuse and not caring for the protection of them are concerned with tourism. If the country not been able to protect natural phenomena in its glory, it is impossible to attract tourist inflow in the country. It is impossible to control the protection of nature by means of legislation only. There must be a vehicle or means to be created to provide information and education to the tourists as well as inhabitants of the country about the value of natural elements and every care must be taken for their protection with care and prudence.

Together with the preceding natural elements, the intrinsic excellence created by the activity of man stands for the other part of the tourist heritage and are equally as important. The values created by the activity of man personate in historical monuments temples, stupas, monasteries, religious edifices and civil architectures. The important places of history and civilisations serve the biggest source of wealth of the tourist heritage.

These are constituted by archaeological excavations, art galleries, museums, archives, libraries, memorials, monuments etc. The popular arts mean town and villages, their houses, folklore customs and rites etc., they also help to the growth of tourism. The traditional events of any country such as popular religious and civil festivals and feasts, exhibitions, sports, meeting, pilgrimage etc. are also the important tourist resources.

An appreciation of natural values in their true essence can be realised only with the basic understanding of their proper upkeepment and not making wastage or damage of free gifts provided to mankind by almighty. In reality, international visitors like to visit and enjoy vacation in the country where there are natural sights with their pristine surroundings not making any obstructions by modern means of developments. We have now noticed that international tourists like to visit ski slopes of the Alps in the winter more than in other places. So the international visitors like to make safaris in Africa. International visitors are lured by the great snowy peaks of the Himalayas of Nepal and they are making travel to Nepal in large numbers. So the values which make up the tourist heritage certain, occupy a prominent position for attracting large number of visitors or tourists in a region of a country. So the international tourists movement tends to concentrate solely in the classic tourist regions but now many are coming to the new regions having attractions unique to them. This is a real fact and was noted in 1937 by the Economic Committee of the League of Nations which narrate :

> "Almost every country possesses a certain variety of climatic and geographical conditions and, on the other hand, a national culture of some value. Each one can, therefore, continually exercise an increasing attraction on foreign tourism."

Each country is more or less touristically attractive and can become one willingly visited by tourists, if it ensures that it can properly make arrangements for visit to such places of attraction easily and assessment is very properly managed.

The development of such tourist resources—natural as well as man's activity—can be made attractive only by making international tourists to visit such places easily. Such places must have accommodation facilities to live and shelter with foodings and necessary services as well as to allow them to enjoy the tourist heritage to the maximum ensuring physical, therapeutic, cultural or moral benefit from it. So this is utmost important to adjust development by means of specialised plant and to be attractive to international tourists in all times to come.

5

PROGRESS IN TRANSPORT

The Principle Element of Tourist Movement

Transport is one of the great requisite and special feature of Tourism. Tourism without movement does not occur and it cannot be carried on living in one place without making a travel. So transport is a characteristic activity within tourism to which a large part of the tourism expense is used.

Travel by walking was the first way of tourist travel in the past. To-day, many kinds of transportation means for travel are available. The means of transport and technique generally denote the essential component of travel. Pilgrims used to travel on foot in the middle ages. The travellers of the Renaissance also travelled for work, business, education, health and also for tourism on foot. It is recorded that the Swiss Toppfer, was the champion of travellers on foot. But now many kinds or means of transport are available and so the people like to travel by those means of travel. In the by-gone years, differences in prices and the availability of fuel have had a direct influence on both the development of tourism and restructuring of the demand. But now, with a clear downward trend in cost of energy prices and greater supply than demand, travellers will have more available income to devote to other expense items, to use better accommodation or, they may simply want to visit tourist destinations further from their place of residence.

Road Transport

For the share of the various modes of transport, land transport, particularly by roads, continues to provide for the greatest share of total international tourist movement. Specially, for Europe and Canada and the United States, the predominant mode of transport is land transport or specifically road transport.

Road transport is very important for travel both for tourists and for nationals of any country. Majority of people travel by road transport. In order to connect the different areas of the country, the predominant mode of transport is land transport. Road transport is essential also to permit visitors to visit the tourist destination which attracts them. So easy transport facilities are one of the prime requisite for attraction of international tourists. Travel to different regions of any country requires good land transport arrangements not only for international tourists but also for domestic tourists. Good land transport helps international as well as domestic tourists to enjoy the tourist heritage to the maximum.

Rail Transport

Rail transport is significant in only a small number of countries. Most of these are in Europe. Two-thirds of the railways are found in Europe and North America. But railway has only insignificant development except in some proportion such as Argentina, India etc. to other parts of the world.

The major role of the railway was to transport heavy merchandise over great distances and this task will remain so in future. In the face of the railway transport of travellers is a public service everywhere and tend considerably to the development of tourism. The railway has now to face fierce competition in order to transport of travellers as a public service everywhere.

The railway companies have to devise a comprehensive policy to face fierce competition with other means of transport. So the railway companies have reckoned to speed, comfort and other good services. Now there are services of inter-urban fast trains at the national and international level. The Trans-Europe Express (TEE) provides an illustrated example for ultra-modern trams run by electric, very comfortable covering a dozen lines connecting many cities of Western Europe. Such types of trams are in use in many developed countries of the world. These trams run covering great distances and generally very comfortable having fully air-conditioned, sleeping cars, wagon-lits, restaurant cars, etc. These are auto-couchette trains which transport motor cars and tourists and allowing the tourists to sleep on board during the night. Such trains are usually used by business travellers.

Some countries having major tourist attractions have developed trams solely for tourist services. These trams services are directly related to tourism and generally such networks used primarily to tourist regions in mountainous areas. The Rack Railway with a supplementary toothed rail and the Funicular (coaches run by cable) is in use in Switzerland operating on routes having beautiful and impressive views not seen in any part of the world.

Other types of railway are Telpher Railways, forms of transport by cable, of lighter construction, usually used for skiers. These are also called mechanical lifts ski-tow, Drag lift etc. and are in use on snow surface in winter.

There are now many rail techniques developed with a variety of systems such as Ferry Boats and Train Ferries which consist of ships specially involved for transportation of railway coaches with passengers. Such services are available Calais-Dover or Ostend-Dover for the channel crossings.

Mono-rails are suspended train running on one track. There are several systems. Most important Allweg is in Japan.

Another train is known by the name of Hovert rain. A train is able to move driven and operated in the air above the surface of sea or land.

As already indicated, passenger rail transport is significant in Europe and to a lesser extent in North America. These countries are even now making efforts to improve the quality of the services offered to travellers in terms of comfort and reduction of travelling time.

Road Transport (Motor Car, Motor Coach etc.)

Since the Second World War, the motor car has become an essential means of tourist transport due to unforeseen developments. Motor Car, which was considered luxury in the past years, has now become an essential item for day-to-day life. There are now a number of motor cars such as private owned by an individual for his personal service, taxis, jeeps etc.

Motor Car has the advantage of modern transport. Road transport by car has flexibility and mobility and freedom of its use. Travel by car can be arranged departure as well as arrival to any place at one's choice and desired time. It also provides comfort, speed and safety. The tourist at motor car can visit any place at leisure and stop and enjoy the views or sight-seeing at his wishes. Due to these advantages, private vehicles are the mode of transport, 80 per cent of the domestic tourism movement in the United States. This privileged position of the private motor car as a mode of transport in tourist travel is in use though there is increase in motor-car utilization costs—consisting of the purchase of a motor-car and fuel, maintenance and insurance costs. Tourists travel by motor car cannot stay longer in any place of tourist attractions as more days than those travelling by rail. The duration of a stay will be less by motor-car tourists and hence there is no increase of foreign exchange earnings to any tourist generating countries and also no more earnings for accommodation sector due to shorter stay of tourists. But tourists travelling by motor car can reach new tourist regions easily if the road conditions are good. It is easier especially for mountaineous regions having tourist resources in plenty to develop tourism by motor cars.

Tourism has a tremendous growth due to the collective transport by Motor Coach. Transport by coach can carry a large number of visitors comfortably even by passing greater distances easily and at moderate costs. Such travel carries the visitors directly to the accommodation of their stay without any inconvenience transfers. So the places having good road networks are becoming popular as well as causing movement of heavy traffic providing arrangement of good management for safety and good services.

Motor or coach tourism rely's more on the condition of the road network. Road should be tar macadam with well signposted and speed should also be checked. Alongwith these facilities there must be provision of lodging, rest houses or lodges, availability of petrol station, road maps and repairing services on the road. The most important matter is the necessity of organising Parking Areas and service stations all along the road. It is dead certain that new road construction is a must for the development of the tourist movement. Tourist transport or passenger transport generally consists of two and four wheeled vehicles which appear to be medium within road transport. In order to development of road transport, the following subjects are to be managed in right ways :

- — Security—Social security and harmonization of the legal regulations relating to motor-car insurance.
- — Regulations for consumer protection,
- — Simplification or abolishment, where possible, of customs and police formalities and controls at borders;
- — Standards to improve road signs.
- — Improvement and expansion of road infrastructures.

There are also mixed transport systems combined with other means of transport : car ferries, auto-couchette trams. Many airlines have started transporting the motor cars of passengers for example air ferries : cross channel, to the islands of Mediterranean.

There are Hovercraft operating on air cushions, carried by different-speed propellers for use on land without roads, swamps, bogs, show etc.

Now Rotel means mobile hotel or sleeping car attached with sleepers and other basic facilities.

There is also caravan, individual trailer with two to six beds and run by a tourist motor car. This type of transport is highly developed in the United State of America and in England. Such transport provides tourists more freedom and easy mobility.

Tourists usually like to use motor cars or coach for tour by larger groups for easiness and very good for visiting different places of attraction without any difficulties and hassels in accordance with their wishes.

Sea Transport

This type of transport is directly related to tourism with the cruise. This type of transport was formerly used in sea, lake or river for transportation of heavy goods. With the development of the cruise the tourists are also now carried by such services. Shipping services operate in certain cases for a tourist service.

It is now essential to know more about Maritime shipping and Inland shipping.

Maritime shipping—Maritime shipping has both kinds of services as to short distance regular lines near to ports and to long distance services to overseas destination. Such services depend upon chosen itineraries and the routes of passage to tourists regions.

The regular shipping lines are regular with density in the Mediterranean and between Europe and the Americas. Along-with these lines, there are also shipping services between Europe—Far East, North America—South America, North America—Pacific islands, Japan—Australia etc. Following some years of definite decline owing to the competition of air transport, even then this mode of travel for tourists has also its own attraction. But while going historical accounts, the coming of scheduled air services and the independence of old western colonial empires have reasonably weaken the role of shipping companies which had flourished very much in 1850 and 1950.

There are other forms of sea transport as Maritime pleasure shipping, cruises etc. Maritime pleasure shipping is special and non-commercial shipping with boats of low tonnage with an arrangement of transferring many passengers (yachts). This type of tourism is amply used in countries with a developed economy with good coastline as Mediterranean countries, U.S.A. etc.

Cruises are usually round-trip trips organised for touristic purposes for a considerable group by shipping companies, ship-owners, travel agencies or tourism associations. They organise travel to tourist areas with variety of attractions for several days with great deal of comfort and safety, arranging transfer if needed.

Inland Shipping—Apart from the forms described above, there are also inland shipping. These services consist of regular lines on lakes, rivers, canals etc. Such shipping lines are used much by tourists. Examples are noticed on the Rhine, the Danube, the Nile, services on the Swiss or Italian lakes.

There are pleasure shippings which are available on request to the visitors along the tourist resorts situated on the water bodies. These pleasure shipping can be enjoyed by paying rent which involve rowing boats, motorboats etc.

Many seasonal cruises an the picturesque routes of Rhine, Rhone, Danube, Mississippi rivers are operated in summer for enjoyment or enjoying unique sights with comfort. There are arrangements also at port of call and visit to sites of attraction, cites and monuments as an organised tour.

Side by side with these shipping means, there are mixed shipping systems such as ferry boats, trainferies, Hydrofoils and crafts, Hovercraft etc. Hovercrafts are regular lines for example between Portsmouth and the isle of Wight and for the crossing of the English Channel.

Air Transport

Air transport has a very promising future The aircraft is the present day means of transport with the highest growth rate. It is the swift way of transport of persons for long distances. The speed and comfort have made air transport an ideal convenience of tourism transport.

The importance of air transport is very much appreciated simply because of speed and free time of which tourists have at their disposal, especially for annual holidays, weekends and other holidays. Specially in inter-continental services, the high speed of the air services lessens the length of flight making length of stay more at the chosen destination. The world tourism has increased tremendously by goodness of inter-continental services. The country or countries located at far and wide distances as geographical demarcations are different now can be approached without difficulty from the tourist movement. Many countries of the world, having no other means of access, can be approached by the aeroplane services.

The aeroplane is a decisive instrument of tourism development in the case of Africa.

Air transport started 60 years before firstly and with the start of supersonic aircraft from 1970, all places on the earth are easily reached in an average of 23 hours. Jet-planes mobilized speed up in travelling which is prompt to go swiftly to circle the earth. It is convenient to go everywhere in the world within 30 hours. The mobilization of 3 mh supersonic plane has contributed to speed up of the world transportation. It is presumed now that in the year 2000 some two thousand million people will take to the air, more tourists from western Europe, North America and Far east. Now it is essential to know about Scheduled Airlines, Charter aircraft and inclusive fares.

Scheduled Airlines—In such airline services the tariffs, the iteration, the standard of comfort and the routes followed are fixed and controlled by international organisation—International Air Transport Association (IATA).

Charter Aircraft—Such airline services are both on scheduled or unscheduled routes. There are flights on request for which tariff structure is independent and assents to the laws of the market. In such a case, it is possible to arrange the transport singly or also travel including accommodation and amusements. Flights of charter aircrafts are reserved on request mainly for independent groups representing a club, a firm or other organised associations.

Inclusive Tour—signifies an all-inclusive air travel. According to IATA definition of a round-trip undertaken in whole or in part by air for an all-inclusive price which covers accommodation of the persons. The tour may also bestow supplementary advantages, use of scheduled airline services or charter of a special aircraft. The price of inclusive travel is regulated throughout the world to bodies—tour agencies or responsible bodies for the sale and in accordance with the legal provisions of a definite contract. All inclusive travel plays an extremely important role in the development of tourism.

The new technique is particularly concentrated on the introduction of supersonic aircraft. It is believed that the aircraft of the future will travel at more than 3,200 km per hour which is 2.5 times the speed of sound.

The Helicopter is also used in air tourism for winter sports in order to link a main airport with ski resorts which can build a helipad. It is also used at present to carry tourists to various mountain resorts for viewing mountain and valleys.

Tourism, prompted by Jumbo Jets Charter tours and the affluence of the industrial nations has become a great economic activity in the present world. So the airline transport has seemed to offer an opportunity to earn foreign exchange and incite economic growth to many developing countries having various natural and cultural resources even without having road transportation. The air transport makes access to countries whose geographical location is difficult, have begin to profit from the tourist movements.

6

THE STATE AND TOURISM

Development and Promotion of Tourism

Tourism has important and close relationship with the activities of the state. The fundamental task of the state is to direct, stimulate and synthesize movements of persons for leisure and holiday purposes as well as for cause of duty or obligation. Movement of international visitor or foreign tourist is regulated by certain rules of each country. Such rules and regulations are formed and enacted by the state authority. Such responsibility flaps on the socio-cultural, economic and political framework of the country concerned and is vested in the National Tourism Administration, which is a Government body with responsibility of movement of persons. Not only the movement of foreign tourists but even the tourist expenditure in foreign exchange is regulated by the Act of the country or state. It is necessary for states, therefore to ensure that tourism policy to which they are assigned, makes necessary provision for the developments of tourism.

Socio-economic importance of tourism is numerous. State and Tourism are associated in many ways. Tourism is very dynamic trade. The way of conducting facilities and services has always to be enhanced. There is competition in this field at all times and so there is need to update by analyzing the demand of the client. So, there is provision to be made generally by the state for the regular survey of the need of clients. Only by assigning itself with survey, helps to know the tourist's trend. Development and promotion of tourism considerably depends on State intervention and support. Such responsibilities have given rights in enacting rules and regulations and policies for tourism. Tourism cannot be developed and promoted without such rules and regulations. So State intervention in tourism is necessary and generally is active in all countries of the world. The state, therefore, has the sole authority for discharging, regulatory and promotional functions as well as policy formulation and their subsequent implementation.

National Tourism Administration : Role of Furelios

In order to co-ordinate the role of tourism activities in the country for adaptation and creation of tourist products and services, such responsibility is vested in the National Tourism Administration in the world with the management of actual development and provision of such products and services giving as a vital function for the operational sector.

There are four main fields in which National Tourism Administration exercises its responsibility for the movement of persons :

(*i*) Research, planning and statistics;
(*ii*) Development and Investment promotion;
(*iii*) Marketing and promotion;
(*iv*) Co-ordination, Standard-setting and Regulation.

With functions indicated above, the National Tourism Administration assumes responsibility for the implementation of a country's tourism policy.

The National Tourism Administration's function of research, planning and statistics will enable suitable types of supply to be attained to meet the requirements of markets, while that of research and statistics in addition to identifying the requirements will ensure the desirability of products and services to be directed and checked. The role in standard-setting and regulation is important for the National Tourism Administration, simply because to ensure that the quality of the products and services being offered fulfil the various requirements of different markets.

For development and investment promotion, National Tourism Administration should encourage and stimulate by following appropriate means to tourism operators and allied associations or organisations of social, cultural and religious tourism as well as those associated with youth tourism and special-interest travel to supply appropriate facilities for their particular market segments. Necessary infrastructural development is a major condition for the development of tourism in the country. In order to develop proper infrastructural development investment promotion, the National Tourism Administration will try mainly to assist the operational sector in such activities through facilitating the co-ordination with other state agencies and to provide necessary infrastructure to enable the operations in the new development areas. Necessary infrastructural development is the pre-requisite for the development of tourism in the country. Joint efforts of private and public sector is equally important for infrastructural development. Government has to plan and move forward for such program and priorities keeping eye on its financial resources. So the private sector can come up and help and assist themselves providing suggestions to government in many ways. It is known to all of us that government can help in creating new infrastructure and providing services which is beyond the capacity of private sector. Government also need to give all necessary assistance and co-operation to private in such a case. This relationship between private and public sector is very delicate and has to be maintained by each sector respectfully. A balanced and healthy tourism development is also a must. It needs, therefore, very careful planning and a very co-ordinated approach. Beauty and attraction are generally associated with one's own culture, heritage, tradition, custom, arts, crafts etc. The extra-ordinary image of the country must be maintained, if the singular and unique attractions of the country are lost and not maintained properly which cause less inflow of tourist in the country. That is why a very careful planning is needed.

The National Tourism Administration is highly concerned with the country's tourism product, including attractions, facilities and services be at par with products offered in other countries of the world. To cope with this problem, high priority is urgently needed on designing a working inventory of key tourist industry, national carrier hotels, travel agents, hospitality, recreational facilities and other services. If such arrangements are made, it is sure to help tour producers to prepare best package tours for upgrading services and facilities. National Tourism Administration must consider the problems for the need for more dynamic destination areas with quality of services and facilities to attract more international visitors to the country.

A regional development strategy for generating employment at local level for distribution of income in less developed areas of the country, constitute one of the policy basis of action programme of the government. The plan helps to create the development of resort areas as one of the important aspects of tourism in the country with the above strategy. This strategy should aim to increase the average length of stay of tourists in the country and to preserve many natural areas in their salvan settings. While developing resort areas in the country, the policy of the government must be to develop resorts in those areas where if possible there is already growth of some tourist infrastructure. Government will invest to build infrastructure in developing resort areas but it is better that it will not compete with private sector activities, while developing resort areas, the national resources such as trees and green should be upkept as in their natural habitat as they could be ornament for the attraction of the country.. If the natural resources are destroyed, the asset of attraction will disappear. So preservation of natural resources and protection of wildlife is generally considered by the government for long-term tourism development. So many governments of various countries now are preserving their natural resources as a must for long-term tourism development. It has been generally an accepted fact that the tourist infrastructure should be constructed by the Public Sector and the other complimentary and supplementary tourist investment should be realised by private sector in the country. The development of low cost facilities and services to cater to domestic travel very often becomes the responsibility of the National Tourism Administration, particularly in the developing countries since the private operational sector regards the rate of return on investment in such facilities and services insufficient.

Politics, Planning Control

Politics, Planning and Control are more or less based on the economic regimes of the different countries of the world. These countries have been largely divided into two main divisions : The countries like U.S.A., Germany, Italy, Switzerland, U.K., Japan are regarded as free regimes. There are socialist countries and USSR as collective regimes. So it is necessary to know the ways in which the economic regimes themselves affect tourism. Policy divisions will determine whether tourism is developed at all, what type of tourism is attracted and the benefits it generates. The planning and control of tourism depends on the socio-political structure of the society of the country which conditions policies on tourism. The countries having Free Regimes have free or collective degree of state intervention in the economy. In such Free Regimes each individual is considered an economic subject, exercising free exchange and state action is limited to prescribing the arrangements which govern the most flexible economic relations between individuals. In the collective, centralised economic regime, on the contrary the state assumes responsibility for all economic possibilities within the framework of its development plans. A few socialist countries, have actively discouraged international tourism for fear of outside influence on their population and the country. But the majority of countries have not adopted the approach as described above and among those which actively promote tourism are many from the socialist and capitalist camps. So the methods in which tourism is organised and its impacts can be expected to differ largely in countries with different political structures.

The state seeks the best possible results from the society. The degree of state intervention in the collective economy is very high. The state regulates or even directly manages, tourist consumption within the framework of the general economic plans. As Emanuel de Kadt mentions in 'Tourism : Passport to Development' book, published by World Bank and UNESCO, Oxford University Press as follows :

> "A comparative analysis of the social and cultural implications of the policies followed by different Eastern European countries with respect to tourists from the West would also be exemplary. The major objective of their tourism policies is to raise the welfare of their citizens by providing appropriate recreational facilities, foreign exchange is only a secondary objective."

In the free economy, the state's task consists of creating the structures and in proposing models for the organisation of tourist industries without imposing production or consumption standards. As this attitude does not mean not a completely discutenested for this activity. The state employs some direction on tourism. The State is not principally concerned with tourism supply and demand but it influences the output, modifies it and then corrects the results. Private activity (hotels, travel agencies) is not carried out independently with mere State Authorisation, but depends on the large public sector. The state fixes the price of electricity or the train fares, it improves the telephone system and the roads and all this has an influence on the private tourism industries. The State's Tourism Policy is governed by the general principle of obtaining the best possible results for the society as a whole.

The role of government in Tourism has a regulatory and when the national interest to be affected. This regulatory action by government should, however, be kept to the minimum level necessary to bring a given situation under reasonable control. Regulatory systems should not be cumbersome or unenforceable where controls can be established without the requirement of legislation, this should be encouraged. As the tourist industry grows, it attracts elements that have short-term profit motives which conflict with long-term national or industry interests. The tourist industry should therefore devote attention to the establishment and effective operation of self-regulatory mechanism, reducing thereby the need for statutory control.

So the consultation between government and industry in the establishment of regulatory system is desirable. So the State will have to take measures to enhance the power authority and responsbilities of their administration with responsibility for the movement of persons, so as to ensure that they carry out their functions in the most effective manner while the role of co-ordinating the adaptation and creation of tourist products and services is the responsibility of the National Tourism Administration, the actual development and provision of such products and services should be a vital function of the operational sector. Given constant increases in travel motivations and forms of travel and the sheer volume that movements of persons will reach if the right policies are pursued, they will then require increased and co-ordinated intervention by the state so as to provide products and services of various kinds for both new and traditional markets.

The importance of tourism is to the integrated development of the economics of the country. Government should take a long-term view in this respect and give high priority to tourism in the national plan so as to ensure allocation of adequate resources.

While making Tourism development, distinction must be made between infrastructures such as roads, utilities etc. and superstructures as hotels, tourist transportation, shops etc. Government has direct responsibility for the infrastructures as road, highway construction as well as utilities but in respect to the superstructures its role should be more oriented to establishing the climate in which the private sector can operate. However, where the private sector does not and Government has to come up and establish infrastructures for the development of tourism at the initial stage and then this involvement ensures as an exemplary action to favour the tourism sector. Where the private sector does not and when government dictates, the government role in respect to superstructure becomes a primary one.

In developing countries, government has undertaken entrepreneurial role to ensure tourism activities. Active involvement is characterized as a deliberate action by the government to favour the tourism sector. Indirect state involvement occurs when government enacts legislations relating to foreign tourist and their movement within the country, their period of stay, state security *vis-a-vis*—frontier formalities, control of foreign exchange earnings through tourism, establishment and management of hotel and other tourist establishment etc. Apart from these, employment of foreign nationals, bilateral and multi-national co-operation in tourism are also direct activities of government.

So by the narration specified above, it is clearly known that various direct and indirect actions of government are involved in tourism sector. The involvement of state is further related with the condition that most developing countries are characterized by a scarcity of resources for developing purposes, where private sector is sky. The most typical areas of state intervention in tourism sector are as follows :

(*i*) Policy formulation and implementation.
(*ii*) Invention of resources and tourist attractions to the country.
(*iii*) Ecological protection and tourist zones.
(*iv*) Establishment of standards and regulations governing tourism activities.
(*v*) Encouragement of private investment in the sector through fiscal and credit measures.
(*vi*) Construction of plant and infrastructures to facilitate tourism promotion and development of tourist resorts.
(*vii*) Drawing up and conducting promotional and marketing campaign.
(*viii*) Technical and Vocational training in tourism.
(*ix*) Research, studies and tourism statistics.

The state has a role to play in tourism training. Having responsibility for general education, it should play its part in training individuals in the necessary skills to adapt existing products and services and to devise and create new products. The tourism training system should help some of its best students to become entrepreneurs and innovators in the field of tourism.

Tourism Revenue

Tourism helps a lot to earn state revenue. The state obtains resources from tourism through public revenues in the same way as they are obtained from establishment of other sectors. Although tourism activities have certain special characteristics, resulting from difficulties in defining the sector and evaluating its economic importance, it is certain that these exist in financial flow of consumptions, investment and income which provide the state with a basis to determine the tax involvement. Of course, state levies tax and obtains revenues from individuals and forms not because of their general activities of production, investment and consumption. Certain consumption activities such as purchase and operation of aircraft, shipping and other transports, purchase of foreign exchange and rental of hotel accommodation etc. are subject to special fiscal provisions and at the same time are specifically tourism activities.

Most state revenues are obtained by applying general taxation to tourist activities. The main elements of such taxation system are as follows :

Different types of State revenue involved in tourism can be coereive revenue by means of fiscal power such as

(*a*) rates for use of tourism services,

(*b*) special contributions derived from tourism activities or services and taxation

   (*i*) direct on income, wealth and personal expenditure,

   (*ii*) indirect on sales volume of specific consumer products on internal circulation of wealth and on external trade (tariffs).

The state has a penal power to impose fines and penalties for contravention of regulation of governing tourist activity or for contravention of the laws of the country in respect of tourism activities. The state also derive contractual revenues from the administration and operation of public property and industry. These constitute revenues on income derived from the use of tourism resources, revenues on net income from the operation of tourism establishments and lastly free revenues which may be obtained from donations.

Among the different forms of revenues, those of fiscal nature are generally the most important. These type of revenues are based on consumptions by tourists and income generated from the sale of tourist products. Fiscal revenues are counted both from direct and indirect, receipts resulting from the effects of tourism on other economic activities.

Factors determining the value of Fiscal Revenue from tourism are :

(*a*) the degree of development of tourism.

(*b*) the tax collecting capacity of the fiscal system—it will be more sophisticated.

Another factor is contributing to social and economic development. Modern tax system is not limited to being simply means of obtaining revenues but it should be purposeful to ensure proper socio-economic development of tourism. The most important factor tax system must be well administered which implies that it should be simple and easy to understand for the tax payer.

Incentives to Tourism

State has also a policy on tax incentives for tourism. Greater incentives are given to tourism. The state provides tax benefits or tax holiday for tourism in the initial phase of tourism development which are evidently aimed at promoting investment, the development of certain areas, employment creation and in general the stimulation of tourism's economic effects. The objective of such a policy is to ensure flow of tax revenues that tourism would generate gradually.

Tourism sector makes a substantial contribution to state revenue. It varies from country to country according to importance of tourism in the national economy and magnitude of tourism's involvement.

State also involves in expenditure in tourism. State activities are directly and indirectly involved in the development and promotion of tourism. Regarding state expenditure and tourism, the following factors are given below :

Financial and Fiscal Policy towards tourism must be based on the prime objective and tax incentives to tourism to increase the rate of investment by improving the prospects of economic returns from tourism investment—selectively promoting investment in specific region, activities or tourist enterprises or by creating projects or services to meet specific social needs.

Taking into consideration the above objectives, the state formulates various policies, rules and regulations for granting financial and fiscal concessions to the private sector through subsidies, lower interest loans, tax concessions, preferential customs duty, preferential land concessions and various other concessions.

The state also allows tax incentives for tourism investment and generally application of these are by way of the following means :

— *Exemption of Tax*. This exemption is generally granted at the initial stage of establishment. It runs from three to ten years, varies from country to country and nature of projects.
— *Allowance granted to tax payers*. Tax deductions are allowed to make up capital losses due to heavy investment in tourism sector by means of accelerated depreciations etc.
— *Tax credits*. These are specific reductions granted either on the value of the tax base or for purpose of determining liability of tax.
— *Tax deductions*. This form of tax incentive is utilized to promote tourism so that consumer prices are lower and consumption by tourists presumably higher.

Expenditure in Tourists

State has also direct expenditure on tourism administration and development. State involvement in tourism is implicated to various expenditures incurred by state management or in public sector. These may be identified as follows :

(*i*) Cost of development and maintenance of place of tourist interest such as archaeological sites, national parks, recreational parks, zoos, museums, beaches, tourist sightseeing places etc.
(*ii*) Cost of infrastructure and super-structure and public utility services used by the tourist;

(*iii*) Operating cost of government establishments in the tourist sector.

(*iv*) Government expenditures on operation of National Tourism organisation, marketing of Tourism, promotional activities, personnel Training and maintenance of training institutes, etc.

(*v*) Fiscal and monetary incentives by way of tax holidays and rebates , duty concessions, investment subsidies, interest rebates, capital participation, operating subsidies etc.

In discharging such responsibilities, the functions, the state has to incur various expenditures for which it has to levy tax on various tourism activities, operations and establishments. As such tourism has much contribution to state revenue in the form of various taxes. Tourism's contribution to state revenue is higher in comparison to other sectors. But the magnitude of investment in tourism is less in comparison to other sectors. The Manila Declaration clearly refers to tourism's cultural, social and even political value in addition to its economic contribution. As such, development and promotion of tourism deserve much more efforts at state level.

7

TOURIST ACCOMMODATION AND TRAVEL AGENCIES

Accommodation in essence are principally tourist enterprises. They are very importantly related with tourism and denote one of the three fundamental frames of Tourism, for example journey stay, amusement that of stay at one's selected place. So the characteristic feature of tourist accommodation is temporary. Housing crisis in big cities has caused to accept permanent guests. At the same time, lodging in caravan homes for professional reasons, at construction sites by the technicians, is not regarded at tourist accommodation. Similarly, temporary arrangements of residence are made for holiday and weekends.

Accomodation and its types

The Hotel industry is one of the oldest professions in the world and it was also referred in the Bible. The tourist accommodation establishments have developed in the Twentieth century by various names and significance. Camping, youth hostels, holiday village, the motel—all these new types of tourist residence came into existence after the second world war. There are instances of mention of villas, castles and pleasure houses made by the aristocracy in all historical periods. Lodging used by the travellers may be divided in various ways into several categories. While making categories of lodging, it is primary important to find out the aim sought whether it is for gathering statistics, investment policy, encouragement of certain types of tourism etc. Anyway, the below described criteria is considerd as essential :

— Economic Importance :
— Classic and traditional establishments (hotels)
— Supplementary establishments (youth hostels, refuges, holiday camps etc.)

While finding the economic importance as stipulated above, it is necessary to find out the type of users i.e. whether it is a commercial establishment—hotels open to all categories of tourists, or a place of lodging of a special nature open on certain conditions—accessible to a limited clientle such as trade union holiday homes, enterprises, camping sites for clubs etc. Alongwith these categories there are also private lodgings attached as secondary residence, weekend bungalow, tents, caravans, yachts etc.

The property belonged to the owner also causes to make the type as family hotel company or property of a body corporate company, transport company, the state etc.

The accommodation establishments are also related with duration and their opening. There are year-round enterprises in big cities. Similarly, there are seasonal enterprises such as summer, winter as well as public holidays. Side by side with season enterprises, there are also one-season enterprises—hotels open in winter in sports resorts.

The comfort and rates of each type of accommodation very much vary in accordance to local conditions. An hotel cannot be compared with a mountain refuge nor can an hotel in France be compared with one in Japan. Comfort varies on a large scale, hotels with private bathrooms, lift, garden and sauna tents with ice boxes and T.V. There are holiday villages with bamboo houses, wooden huts or bungalow and simple or luxury caravans etc.

The accommodation establishments also depend on geographical localisation as for example in mountaineous areas, rural, cities, forests, beaches etc.

The usage of all such establishments depend on the wishes of the stay of the travellers. The usage for stay is also organised for groups for a limited time of a week, a month etc. Family guest houses take guests for duration of their holidays. There are also certain motels which limit the stay to two or three nights.

The construction of the accommodation establishments are solid in the case of hotel, chalet, villa etc. and mobile or collapsible for tent or boat caravan.

The size and volume of such establishments will generally depend on each type of accommodation as well as the country. An hotel of 100 beds is considered as a big enterprise and a holiday camp for 100 children as a small enterprise.

The Hotel Industry :

The hotel generally refers a house for accommodation of strangers. This is a commercial establishment proposed to provide strangers with lodging, food and other services associated with them. The word 'hotel' also signifies an inn in France, also a public office, private town-house, a palace etc. The hotel de villa means a townhall and hotel-Dieu refers to a hospital. Anyway, the term 'hotel' is very popular in the present world which denotes accommodation establishments providing a certain degree of comfort.

The characteristic phenomena of hotel is : *firstly*, it is a fixed, constructed installation in the form of a building. It provides lodging services to all public except unaccompanied minors (children). So hotel is an enterprise which sells goods and services necessitating payment of the cost needed to reimburse general charges and substantiate an adequate profit. Financial autonomy is a characteristic trait of an hotel enterprise.

But now some countries have provided subsidies, necessary fiscal advantages to boost up hotel business and assist it to earn profit. So an hotel should be able to supply individual services for a person as well as for a family or a group. It provides uniform overall services of average or superior quality such as rooms with or without bath, meals at different prices, dry-cleaning, laundry, sale of postcards and souvenirs, tobacco and variety of drinks, etc.

Hotel is classified into several categories taking consideration of certain aspects which are :

Firstly, to the degree of comfort, the degree of equipment, the volume of services and the cost of services given.

Secondly, the duration of operation is considered whether it is for one season, two season or the entire year.

Thirdly, the purpose of its services and its situation as it is located in cities, mountains, seaside, spa, resorts, transit points etc.

Fourthly, size is also regarded as one essential element for category of an hotel. The American style hotel is categorized by the number of rooms and European style hotel by the number of beds.

Hotel classification system is universally recognized for the notice of the public as well as to authorities. The classification system have been used by several countries but the classification clauses differ from one country to another.

A draft of International classification suggested by International Union of Official Travel Organisations (IUOTO) and proposing five main categories : Luxury, 1st, 2nd, 3rd and 4th was approved by 62 member countries of the organisation in 1965.

The hotel is also an instrument of production. The hotel is also like any other business, an enterprise for the production of goods and of services intended to be sold for a profit to remunerate the administration and the capital involved. The production of goods depends usually in the form of food stuffs into different dishes and meals served to clients. It is also a unit of wholesale trade when it sells alcohol, drinks, cigarettes, postcards etc. It provides services by renting rooms, if necessary other services of hall, lounges, swimming pool, garden, sporting installations, children parks, banquet and conference halls etc. In economic terms, the hotel is a complex productive unit exercising several functions of reception.

The hotel is a complex productive unit so it functions on the very technical ways and on the organisation of a certain type of competence and specialisation. So it more or less depends among the qualified employers and workers. The prime services of a good hotel are concerned with proper and well-managed direction, reception, cuisine, restaurant, bar, floors, rooms, hall, stores etc.

The mission of hotel industry is (1) Lodging-Privacy, and (2) Food and Beverage. While dealing with lodging principally there are two matters—(*a*) the quality of service must be good and proper to satisfy the travellers, and (*b*) counter-measures for noise for the accomplishment of privacy. Side by side with lodging, food and beverage must be hygienic as well as clean. In the past, hotel used to serve drink without alcohol. After the 20th century the proportion of beverage has been used up to the present. Generally, emphasis of the good hotel runs as Room 40%, Food 40%, Bed 12% and others 8%. Anyway percentage of food and bed accounts to 52%. Since after the 20th century, the hotel has been paving the load for more services for food and drinks for the tourists. The characteristic of a hotel is service—the personal service, uniformed service means waitress, bell boys or doorman. It is a service of a man with a uniform. Service is everything behind it. A good hotel always follows the ideal as "Custom is first, Life is service."

We have specifically described about the characteristics of a hotel. Now it is important to know about some specialised hotel establishments. There are hotel accommodation establishments of a special character devoted to certain types of Tourism. They can be described as follows :

Motel—Such accommodation establishments, are hotels which are established for the purpose of meeting especially the needs of tourists travelling by car. The most developed motel network is in North America. But the difference between a motel and an hotel is not very marked in Europe as well as in other countries of the world.

More functional types of accommodation is met by motel than the classic hotel in the autoroutes. The development of autoroutes causes to a swift service for travellers passing through these routes. So the motel is for the arrangement of situation quite different and so the construction, the technical equipment, the sanitary installations are all arranged accordingly. The restaurant service is busy and operates service of hot meals —day and night. The car owner can park his auto in front of his room and uses only the necessary luggage etc.

Another type of hotel is known by the name of Hotel GARNI and provides only rooms and breakfast. Such type of hotel is usually located in big cities for meeting the needs for passing travellers.

Hotel Pension—Such hotel is generally a small enterprise to service for a clientele staying for a certain period of time with advance notice. Such accommodation has a more or less family character.

There are hotels for conferences or seminars. Such hotels are established around big business cities. Such hotels have halls with audio-visual equipment, material for secretariat, hostesses, duplicating machines and other facilities. HOOK MANOR is a model of this type in Sweden and has a private aerodrome for businessmen.

Outside the traditional hotel industry, there are a number of other installations able to offer to tourists lodging, food and other necessary services. Such lodging facilities provide modest comfort at reasonable rates. They are near the lovely natural environment. They are good for social contact and amusements with more freedom for the traveller to the organisation of the day and dress.

By making casual observation, it is known that there are two groups of tourist accommodation in the present times. These are organised in collective forms such as Holiday Villages, Family holiday homes, Youth hostels, youth centres and colonies, refuges, chalets, homes etc. Another form is family or individual free types such as camping, caravanning, renting of villas, studios and apartments, secondary residences.

Now it is useful to know something about the two groups of tourist accommodations described above.

Holiday Village—The development of holiday villages came into establishment after the second world war. The chief characteristics of such type of villages are related to nature, sports and social events as prime activities. Lodging is provided in such villages all-inclusive for a week or two week at prices which include accommodation, food and amusements. The comfort is very modest because of stay at bungalow, huts, tents etc. Such villages have important reception capacity to 500-1000 persons. Such villages are promoted by important clubs such as club Mediterranee, Tourist Organisations—Touropa,

Populans etc. The famous villages are Mediterranean, the Caribbean warm seaside.

Family Holiday Homes—Such homes also came into existence after the second world war. This type of accommodation is offered by non-profit making organisations and has developed very much in the modern world. Generally Trade Unions are the promoters of such family holiday homes for the use of workers and their families under certain conditions. Such homes are created by sports organisations, clubs etc. The stay may be of a week for groups and limited by certain conditions. Such homes are contracted individually or by clubs and so they constitute a considerable part of Social Tourism.

Youth Hostels—Such hostels are established to facilitate tourism of young boys and girls. The period of stay in such hostels is limited, the price low and naturally the comfort is modest. The food in such hostels is prepared by the users. Such hostels are created for the development of Youth Tourism and are managed and controlled by non-commercial organisations.

Holiday Colonies—Such colonies are created and directed by non-profit making organisations. The structure of such accommodation is light consisting of wood, tents etc. for children and seasonal tourists. The children have common premises and service for meal, amusement, sports etc. Such colonies are controlled by the State for educational or health value. Industries, trade unions, private firms, family associations, church, religious groups, municipalities have also created such colonies for the children of their personnels or related people.

Mountain Refuges and Chalets : Such establishments are created at high altitudes with necessary minimum equipment. Such buildings also provide shelter, food, medicaments and supplies etc. to the mountain-climbers in case of need. The refuges and Chalets are built and run by Alpine clubs, touring clubs and sports associations.

Classes in the Mountains or at the Seaside :

There are school classes which are generally organised at

the mountains or the seaside for a month. Such classes assist students their studies as well as to engage in extra-curicular activities with the assistance of their teachers and coaches. They organise classes in the open air enjoying the natural panorama outside. Such classes are very important for health reasons as their are plenty of opportunities for sports of many kinds for amusements and relaxation far from the urban settings.

The following are private, individual or family type of accommodations.

Camping : A site of collection of temporary dwellings which are pitched by tent or tents on the ground. Campers have to pay an admission fee for the use of grounds. The degree of comfort varies and public services such as toilets, recreational rooms, a restaurant and a grocer's shop are provided. Camping sites must abide by certain government regulations. Camping has now developed in the developed countries and it is at the stage of beginning in the developing countries. If camping is organised in the high mountain areas or in the valley it is known as wilderness camping. In such a case no facilities are provided and the camper's have to take care of all their needs. The camper has to carry his supplies and transports his equipments. Camping was originally used by hikers on foot carrying a Knapsack, but now car camping is in use in the developed countries where there is provision of road everywhere.

Caravanning : This can be defined as a house on wheels. The user pulls a trailer or caravan behind his car which is equipped with cots for sleeping and with cooking and living facilities. So it is similar to car camping. The caravan can be used for safe dwelling in case the weather is bad. Caravanning is becoming successful throughout the world. Caravanning started in England firstly in 1920 and it started immediately afterwords in the United States due to the good road network.

Furnished Seasonal Accommodations : These accommodations are privately owned rooms, apartments, studios, villas and chalets—which are rented usually in cities, towns, in the countryside, in the mountains or at the seaside for holidays. These holiday accommodations are one of the major supplementary means of accommodation.

After accommodation there are restaurants which serve foods and beverages to the visitors. They are commercial establishments. They are established usually to cater to the public. They serve both the local inhabitants and the customers coming from outside. The international visitors are an appreciable source of income for restaurants.

The accommodation are of both types—single-purpose or multi-purpose plant. Single purpose plant is for the exclusive use of tourists. Multi-purpose plant is set-up not only for tourism but it contributes to an increase in its receipts—for example restaurants and grocer's shops etc.

There are chain system of hotels in the world. The most famous chain of hotels in the world are Hilton, Sherton. Hilton rules the world over in hotel business and management. It is foretell for the development of the chain systems of the hotels. These chain hotels are famous in the world simply because of important reasons as :Effective Management—*i.e.* Publicity Sales, Booking throughout the agencies in the world in their own hotels. They are specialist in each field—buying and distributing. Stability of the accommodation as they systematize the management of the hotel agreement of the contract among hotels under one Flag.

By analysis, it is clear that tourism industry is based on an infrastructure available in the country and developed to cope with the demands for the future. Transport and accommodation form two most important factors of the infrastructure and the base for growth of tourism-accommodation for travellers is basically provided by hotels. Other means of accommodation, for example, youth hostels, rest houses, camping sites etc. are supplementary to hotels and their contribution is insignificant. Hence, data about hotels is very necessary for a country's Tourism organisation, both for catering to the needs of tourists, whether foreign or domestic, and for preparation of development plans for the future. It is in this context that an efficient and viable hotel and catering industry is in the frontline of tourism development.

TRAVEL AGENCIES, TOURIST OFFICES AND TOURIST RECEPTION OFFICES

Travel agency is an occupation of initiative and responsibility and without which there can be no genuine place for it in the development of tourism. To do its business, the travel agent must see for itself that he is recognised by public authorities, *(i)* in importance, *(ii)* its elements and *(iii)* by the public, its competence as a creater, a producer with its indispensable profit margin and not occupy the position as underestimate as it is understand of a gratuitous intermediary, a commissionary, a position which vary meanly on all occasions one residues the one ascribed to it. Thus travel agency is a profit-making business firm set up for the purpose of organising trips.

The task of the travel agency is to conjecture beforehand the part of—invest, sell and guarantee—in the problems currently raised by the development of tourism. So it acts on two ways—(1) As middleman between their customers and the firm providing the essential services—transport companies, hotels, entertainment, or (2) as actual tourist entrepreneurs.

The travel agency conducts its activities in two ways—

(1) It works as a middleman and charges commission on individual services supplied by a hotel, a transport company, an impresario *etc.* which are sold to the client by the travel agency. The travel agency acts as a go-between the consumer and producer. In this case, consumer is the tourist and the producer is the tourist enterprise.

(2) It also works as an organiser and sets on its own initiative and at its own risk tours for its customers. It completely plans the fixed itinerary and the modes of transportation, the means of accommodation, the excursions and the entertainment to a specific duration. It organises a complete trip in catalogue at an all inclusive prices. This, being the tour managed by the travel agency at its own cost, it charges the usual commission from the producer (hotel, transport company etc.) and also adds a profit margin to the cost.

It is not necessary now to bring back to memory the life and history of Thomas Cook, as it had to receive the earlier calls. But now the time has changed. The travel agent has to fulfil various demands of the client in modern world. So the travel agent is an informer being possessed of right documentation and go-between for the filling of transport and accommodation. To take into account his promotional effort, and the important services, the allied carrier's and hoteliers—granted a small commission to the intermediary.

The work of travel agency has opened out the development of tourism. There is no trade as it is, which advanced by twenty five million times in less than hundred years. The evolution of transport from the short-winded puffing Billies at road and rail of the beginning of the 20th century were succeeded less than sixty years later by the boundless types—cars of all powers, coaches with many sizes and capacities, and always bigger super-express trains. The present exploits of technological innovation in transports and the airlines programmes for 1971-72 are equiped for a daily five thousand seats.

So the duty of travel agent is very immense in the present world of tourism. A travel agency helps in saving time as it always remains in constant touch with quick telex, fax connections with all areas of tourist activities and so the bookings can be made easily. It provides high quality services, simply because of its constant association with tourist enterprises and the firm belief in a high standard of services.

The travel agency forecasts and accordingly define the market and values its development, to an special extent by taking part in the study of the programmes of the highest parts—aviation in particular—which always precede and give rise to tourism. It exerts an active influence on the suppliers of various services, i.e. transport, accommodation, food *etc.* and look after the best quality of services. It also tries to meet the new requirements of tourist traffic. In such a way, it becomes an active middleman between supply and tourist demand. They must invest and plan the means of coping up with the demand.

Travel agency guides the tourist traffic towards tourist areas. It attempts to sell not only present finished products which may be procured by tourism in its various manifestations and also to face up to the competition of the numerous activities which are originated by the age of leisure. It guarantees since no product is now sold which is not escorted by a guarantee of good performance and good finish. Thus the activity of travel agency is essentially universal and it knows no barriers.

Travel agency plays a greater part in influencing the length of the tourist season, travel during the off-season. It enlarges the tourist market by placing special trips to certain groups of tourist—in specific trips.

A sagacious procedure of improvisation after 1950 by the progress of air transport, economic progress, reduction in working time and the generalisation of paid holidays have changed, radically and suddenly all the factors. The travel agents will avail themselves ready for the immediate future, a future boom filled with Jumbo Jets, and SST's. In the Jumbo age, the travel agents cannot remain the commissioned intermediary but must have their quality of a creater, of a producer. It is not proper ,to think the travel agent as a philanthropic or cultural institute. Supersonic aircraft, in larger and larger numbers and with bigger and bigger capacities, now are able to carry crowds. Motorways equip the means for swift transport between large towns and cities. The proliferation of cars call for travel. The railways make good use of their means and capacity for reception. But this big investment for the development of holiday camping sites, winter resorts and other kinds of activities, on the one hand and for the framing of all adequate means of transport on the other, information and preparation planning these purposes at the management of holiday makers are strived to correspond, but without there ever being or almost never being any combination between the different related sectors. The transport and the hotel industry generally enjoy the advantages of international agreements of reciprocity—the laws dealing with travel agents, the definition of their obligations and their plight varies widely from one country to another with free exercise or licence obligations or state monopoly. Travel agency is becoming the world's vital industry, whose present development, as we have seen, perceived almost unlimited.

Tourist Offices : A Tourist Reception Offices :

Tourist Offices and Tourist Reception Offices are essential for modern tourism. Unlike travel agencies, these offices do not indulge in commercial transactions. They are not selling agents and so do not sell and do not organise trips. Their sole purpose is to supply information about the tourist features such as access, resources and other attractions of a country or the places of tourist sites in the country and to help and assist the visitor. Their prime activities are to supply authentic detailed information to the visitors wishing to visit a country. Such offices are located as near as possible to such potential customers which are generally in a capital of a country, large cities. Such offices are also opened at points of arrival as airports, harbours, railway and bus stations, frontier posts in order to attract visitors to the point of tourist attractions.

In order to man and manage reception and information offices, competent and qualified officers are required. These officers must have full knowledge of all subjects in which the visitors are interested : about the country or places of tourist attraction. They should must speak several foreign languages thoroughly. They also disseminate publicity materials. Such persons must have degree of proficiency from the schools of tourism. Employment, manpower and staff problems are extremely important since such essential offices cannot be utilized without qualified staff. Employment and vocational training, therefore from part of tourist supply. These offices are situated in both generating and receiving areas. They act as effective representatives and public agencies for the countries concerned. They work as a part of a national tourist offices of the countries concerned.

8

TOURISM AND ECONOMY

Tourism as an economic force secures income and employment and improves national balance of trade. There are various economic benefits of tourism which are as follows :

1. Tourism as a source of foreign exchange earner;
2. Tourism as a growth industry;
3. Tourism as a spur to employment;
4. Tourism as a development dispenser;
5. Tourism as a factor in environmental protection;
6. Tourism as a roadway to better understanding etc.

Tourism has important activity for many countries both developed and developing. It attributes contribution of foreign exchange thereby creating situation for favourable balance of payment, contribution to government revenues, development activities for employment and income generation. It has also social, cultural, recreational and environmental activities which too have economic and financial implications. These factors stimulate investment in tourism sector particularly for creation of various facilities like hotel, motel, transport, recreation, various infrastructure and super-structure. The creation of all these facilities entails a huge investment which consequently generate further economic activities thereby growing the economy.

It is known to all of us that tourism is not of course, considered as the main productive factor. It has no doubt, difficulties concerning to quantitative measurement of its contribution to the production. It consists an aggregate of services and products from many other sectors of the economy. The multiform character of tourism is its deception in determining its supply and demand pattern. The deceit is identified as the principal factor for its not being considered as an independent sector in the economic activity as well as in national accounting system. There is no pure identification as to which activity constitute tourism sector. Though social, cultural, recreational and environmental factors are predominant in tourism, even then the effects on these factors cannot be quantitatively measured so as to quantify net economic impact of tourism on the national economy.

Tourism and Economics are very intimately related because the relationship is always expressed by means of tourism's contribution to economic development. Economics is generally identified as a subject by which human beings satisfy their wants for scarce goods and services with socially organised ways.

Tourism is a subject which causes the transfer of capital from one country to another through the movement of tourists who travel for a determined tourist 'product' they have aspired to own by paying costs to it. Tourists are on-the-spot consumers of the complex of services and goods that are offered in a certain destination. As tourism affects various sectors of the economic system of a tourist receiving country through its consumption and investment aspects, so its multiplier effect is higher than other sectors of the economy. So tourism embodies a wide support of productive cycles.

Tourism in the National economy is related with tourist activities and expenditure. In order to know about the phenomenon of tourism in the national economy, quantitative analysis is to be made. This can be done by two ways as Micro and Macro-economic aspects. As narrated above, the relations between tourism and the national economy are many and complex. They have three main features which may be presented as follows:-

Micro-Economic aspects concern with static aspects—tourist demand and supply and market patterns. Tourist supply and the market which has two elements of the market. In economic terms and in the widest term the market is the theoretical meeting point of Supply and Demand. So the market means the combination of transactions of sale and purchase and expresses the adjustment between production and consumption. The total of transactions in liberal economy determines or influences prices. The market always includes two essential elements—a supply and a demand. In the absence of one of them the market does not exist. The supply is the quantity of goods or services which can be sold in the market at a given price. The demand, on the other hand, is the quantity of goods or of services which clients are disposed to purchase at a determined price, taking into account the general average of prices at the time of their decision.

There are several types of market which can be distinguished as :

(a) According to extent of their scope (surface): local, regional, domestic, International market.
(b) According to the nature of goods and services: cotton market, wheat market, labour market, gold market, tourism market etc.

The service market differs considerably from a consumer goods market. So tourism market is characterised by certain specific traits. In tourism, the service is provided where the consumer is found at a given moment. One has to visit India to view Taj Mahal at Agra. Other example, guides and interpreters must be provided at the right moment for services not before and not after for tourism.

Tourist supply is very particular. The tourism market is also associated with the same principles as for all other types of market. But tourism market has certain peculiarities as indicated below:

(a) Tourist services cannot be stocked. Skiing is done when there is snow; it is impossible to preserve snow while waiting the arrival of skiers.
(b) The tourist resources are fixed (localised) and it is the tourist himself who comes to enjoy them
(c) The consumption of touristic services is made possible by travel that is by the journey of the consumer from his home to the tourist resources.
(d) The 'Tourist Service' is a combination of economic (measurable) and non-economic (immeasurable)

goods. Tourism can be expressed by gallons of petrol, by kilometres of railway, by Kilograms of meat or preserves which are consumed and measured. But, there is, in addition, in tourism, the pleasure of the eyes (in museum), the pleasure of the body (in a swimming pool), cultural emotion (at a historical site) which cannot be measured in an arithmetical fashion.

(e) Tourist services are highly specialised (transport, acommodations, recreation etc. In most cases, tourists themselves must resort to various 'specialised markets' for the satisfaction of their needs, such as transport, sleeping accommodation, recreational activities, meals etc.

(f) Tourist supply has a relatively low degree of elasticity, most tourist plant meets only a single need. Such plant is used only by tourists (ski-lifts, pleasure boats etc.)

The tourist market is dynamic and localised. It offers wide range of goods and services to an increasingly large clientele.

A century ago tourists were content to visit spas and places of archaeological interest. Now they have discovered skiing and skin-diving, taken up sailing and riding and expect by the year 2000 to make inter-planetary trips. The geographical relations between tourist supply and demand may take various forms.

Dynamic aspects of Micro-Economic aspects include firms, investments, financing and growth policies. Static aspects constitute estimate of the nation's tourist capital, tourist activities in quantity and value, description of relation between industries that link tourism with the rest of the economy.

Dynamic Aspects: short and long-term trends in tourist consumption, production and capital; seasonal, economic and structural problems in the development of tourism.

The developed countries with a high standard of living consume more tourism then others. Tourist consumption is only possible where there is a high national income.

Tourist countries, *e.g.* Austria, Belgium, Ireland, Italy, Switzerland and Yugoslavia—the receipts from international tourism represented more than 50% of the total tourist receipts inside the country. This demonstrated the importance of international tourism for the tourism industries of these countries, especially in respect of hotels and transport. These countries 'Export' tourism and have an interest in developing a welcoming policy to increase the influx of foreigners. Nations as different as Switzerland and Yugoslavia are making tourism a branch of their export industries.

The effects and influences of tourism are presented on three distinct elements such as *(i)* tourism and the balance of payments; *(ii)* Internal effects, and *(iii)* Influence on general objectives.

Tourism and the Balance of Payments

The balance of payments means all the accounts which a country keeps (income and expenditure) with regard to trade with other countries. The income consists amongst other things capital investment in land, often agriculturally unproductive.

Tourism allows savings to be spent on travel, cruises, visits to art centres or in health resorts, visits to international sports events and cultural festivals etc. Due to the reasons placed above, redistribution of money is made which permits direct increase in employment and a reduction of unemployment in other sectors and also allows a start to be given in the development of under-developed zones.

Tourism is also a growth industry. It is an instrument for achieving general economic objectives within a country's economic life. Tourism helps to facilitate and accelerate the development of a region. It also combats unemployment where labour is in good supply. It brings in foreign currency as an invisible export to improve the trade balance. It helps much to make less the burden of foreign aid on public funds. Lastly, it attracts capital which people do not know where to invest.

Tourism is a tool for regional development. This usually depends on a medium-term forecast of the level of the overall tourist demand (national and international) and take into account the probable importance of the site or of the region of the country which is proposed to be developed as tourist site.

Tourism, at the same time combats unemployment where labour is available and unemployed. So tourism provides a solution to problems of regional development and social promotion, by obtaining the standards required for tourism workers and determining the effect of tourism on all tourist jobs on non-tourism jobs.

Developing tourism as an export is very necessary for the developing countries desiring to obtain industrial equipment and to create, in this way, the general conditions for independent growth. It is the main source of foreign exchange and an important factor in the development of industry and international trade for many countries.

Tourism is also a growth industry. The tourist industry is a composite of several and varied industrial, commercial and government activities. Communications, transportation, accommodation, food, recreation, clothing and other equipments are but a few of the almost innumerable range of services and supplies involved. Tourism as a development dispenser, a high level of co-operation between the elements of the industry, is essential and to achieve this, well management and organisations are required. Many things in this regard has yet to be done. There are heartening signs of advances in these fields. In such a way, a deficit in the trade balance is corrected by importing foreign currency (invisible exports).

Developing tourism as an export a percussion is to be thought of. It is better to attract very rich tourists from the tourist generating markets of the world and to provide them with high class services. Wealthy tourists will naturally bring in more foreign exchange than low income tourists while considering this objective, it is to be considered about the possible repurcussions of wealthy class tourists on the balance of payments of the country. The rich tourist usually consume products of imported varieties which will cause just the reverse effects expected from the import of foreign currency and its real value of importation will be highly diminished. Such activities will also help to cause the habits for the local population for using the high imported brands of products for their uses. Such habits will cause the importation of foreign currency by the tourists completely neutralised. The balance of payment defect may even be increased by importing many luxurious products.

Tourism makes to help in progress for regional expansion. Generally tourist areas are economically not so progressed and have few production sources. But tourism uses goods which have no industrial or agricultural value: Snow (for winter sports), the sand along the sea shore, forests and deserts (national parks). These elements which are unproductive for other industries represent a source of wealth for tourism. Vast areas of land, unsuitable for agricultural development are devoted to leisure and become excellent "Outdoor Recreation Areas" as in U.S.A.

Tourism reorganises public finance by increasing public income by taxation and so the public budget based on insufficient economic activity will be compensated by the promotion of tourism. The subsidies and assistance given by developed countries and international funds as aid loans are reduced and the ratio of debt eliminated.

Tourism also attracts available capital. Many tourism projects lack capital for development. But the private investment always looks for comfortable atmosphere than for public investment. So the state should encourage private sector for the creation and exploitation of tourism installations by providing administrative Fiscal (exemptions) or financial (grants, credit) facilities. In addition, exploitation may also be made easier by credit for modernisation or enlargement of tourist establishments, tax reimbursement. These form a real tourism. The setting up of the general infrastructures depends almost entirely on the public authorities. However, the role of the private sector is very often also affected by the influence of planning and so proper guidance and co-operation should be given for private sector.

Tourism helps much in the redistribution of the national income. Tourism assists in creating new opportunities to utilize and thus prevents the national income being accumulated by a privileged few. Savings were converted into gold, silver, jewels and precious metals in the middle ages. Savings in later ages in Europe were invested in the purchase of land and forests. But tourism on the other hand, allows to veritable exports of goods and services at the present time in the form of sales of national goods and services to tourists who visit the country and pay with foreign currency, help the entry of foreign capital. The expenditure includes, amongst other things; import of goods and services and therefore the tourist expenditure of nationals abroad, the export of national capital which is invested on a short or long term basis abroad.

Internal Effects

Internal effects of tourism for intense tourist demand are as follows :-

Stimulation of employment. The tourist demand increases the level of employment by creating new jobs in the sector. This also stimulates the creation of new activities in other branches such as the building and transport industries. It directly raises the productivity level of other sectors especially that of agriculture, for under-employed or seasonal labour is drawn on tourism sector. The effect in the building industries is considerable, for tourism calls for the construction of many types of buildings, hotels, guest houses, homes, chalets, retreats, residential blocks, group accommodation, holiday villages etc. Innumerable rooms have to be built and to be upkept. The upkeep of these construction which constitute capital investment, provides work for numerous craftsmen.

Tourism being composed of many kinds of services, *e.g.* guides, porters, barmen, drivers, instructors which require a large labour force which must be increasingly skilled.

Tourism creates a new market for certain products. Tourists are interested to purchase on-the-spot (purchase) of national products while visiting tourist sight-seeing places. This is really a very real export trade with no transportation charge for the exporter and which is also exempt for that reason from the risks of international trade. Certain products are especially sought after by the tourists.

Tourism will contribute to the development of other industries such as handicrafts (weaving, embroidery, leather goods, woollen items, jewellery, pottery, food and beverage.) So, it is not only the source of foreign exchange but it helps much to the basic transformation of the country's economy from traditional agriculture to a more modern economy. It will continue to require the development of infrastructure such as adequate transportation systems, water supplies and sanitation facilities. These developments benefit the local residents as well and assist by reducing transportation cost between markets. Tourism has long been regarded an attractive means of economic development. It is a labour-intensive industry which in addition to stimulating direct employment also spreads benefits throughout the entire economy by affecting service and construction sectors which greatly stimulate the demand for local products and capital. In such a way, tourism also attracts available capital as greater dependence on local private enterprise to provide a spectrum of ancillary services to the tourism industry. The business community is a principal beneficiary of increased travel and tourism activity. To enhance attractiveness to visitors, businesses must make both individual and concerted efforts to allure travellers by proper investment of both capital and service on a continuing basis.

Tourism is also considered as a development dispenser. As we know that tourism is composed of very varied consumptions. The tourist pays for his airfare, car, accommodation, sight-seeing, meals, drinks, entertainment and for the purchase of souvenirs. All these activities help much for inter-industry exchanges and assist the value of these purchases. So the economic value of tourism is immense. It means net income for the tourism establishments and other relating enterprises getting in touch with it. It also helps to increase the employment and related enterprises. So if balance of payment in the field of trade is not favourable, tourism may help to improve the balance of international payment. So the countries all over the world are taking measures for the development and promotion of tourism. Now tourism development is becoming the national policy of many countries of the world. In other words it aims at the improvement of invisible income by being a development dispenser.

A tourist is one who makes journey away from his home for business, pleasure, personal affairs. Therefore, the supply aspect of tourism can be defined as the sum of those business enterprises that provide goods and services to tourists. This means the country's economy which signifies the total of all the trade and industry which is carried on in the country. Tourism is considered also as one of the life target in the consumption. Tourist industry in general, effects intensely the local economy. Internally it affects the levelness of wages. Externally the international visitors will bring in foreign exchange. Tourism causes multiplier effect, simply because of many supporting industries attached to it in the production of goods and services.

But it is not proper to say the overall tourism industry as a sum of various industries, since many enterprises offer goods and services to markets other than tourists. Tourism should not be planned or developed for in isolation. So the need to plan for tourism industry in the context of other economic activities, there is also a need to integrate development planning. It provides direct employment to many people in the travel industry, transport, travel business, entertainment, souvenirs and also the indirect employment generating of them.

Influence on General Objective

Tourism is also a factor in environment protection. The conservation of the country's national, historical and cultural heritage is necessary to the growth of tourism. Tourism, itself can be the source of the revenue necessary for conservation. Many of environmental resources are potentially destroyed by the influx in international trade. So the unproper, irrational and disorderly utilization of the environmental resources, whether it may be natural or cultural should be protected of being destructive and injurious in the name of unreal economic development. The sudden growth in tourism has saturated many extraordinary sites and has resulted in the rapid expansion of a tourist infrastructure at the expanse of the environment. Good planning and management are needed from the government, public and private bodies for the continued co-operation, interaction and broad thinking. These activities will help for proper planning and direction as to which quality environment are created for both inhabitants and tourists. The problem of the protection of environment exceeds the limit of legislation. It extends to the field of information and education of tourists as well as all inhabitants without exception.

Tourism is also a roadway to better understanding. International tourism favours contact with civilizations, circulates new ideas, contributes to widening of horizons, to a change in taste and customs and develop the technique of trade and industry.

Tourism is the fundamental and most desirable human activity worthy of commendation and encouragement of all people and all governments. So, it is termed as one of the most laudable human activity. Besides, generating economic activity, it evolves international goodwill and understandings. While developing many industries, tourism creates friendship and expands understanding amongst nations. Tourism is a medium through which we can exchange knowledge and create understanding among the people of the world.

Tourism provides a direct knowledge and contact with the great achievement of the human mind. So it helps to unravel the basic similarities of human feelings with reference to the country and culture. It gives the oneness of feeling which provides a permanent and a fast colour impression of friendship and communicates goodwill far beyond the reach of the mass-media of modern method of education. Socially and culturally, it is a product which leads to the pursuit of intellectual curiosity amongst peoples and nations, a healthy respect of one-another's beliefs and customs and most important tolerance towards cultures different from one's own. Thus it becomes a powerful factor in social achievements and for peaceful relations between nations. International tourism, a broad exchange of peoples by visiting one-another, is one of the most effective means to promote international co-operation and understanding.

9

TOURISM PLANNING

Tourism is an expanding industry in modern world. There is a growing recognition of the importance of the tourist industry throughout the world. It is the main source of foreign exchange earning and an important factor in the development of industry and international trade. International Tourism fosters the development of an international society with deep social and cultural consequences, in association from its economic effects.

There is a spectacular growth of tourist trade in the world at the present time. The growth has been created by such economic and social changes as higher level of employment, higher wages, shorter working hours, increased annual leave and long service leave and security benefits for sickness, unemployment and old age. These benefits have accelerated the accumulation of greater wealth, more leisure time and need for recreational vacation. The improved travel facilities of the present time had helped much for the expansion of tourist business. It is sure to foretell that this tourist business and its expanding trend will go on further expanding in the coming years.

Tourist industry is a composite of many and different industrial, commercial and governmental activities. Lots of services and supplies are involved such as communication, transportation, accommodation, food, recreation, clothing and other necessary equipments.

For the effective development of the tourist industry, a well thought planning and a high level of co-operation between the elements of the industry is essential; and to achieve this, good management, leadership and organisation are required. There are increasing advances in these fields, yet much have to be done for the future.

Planning is concerned generally with the future implications of current decisions. So the basic questions are linked up with the need for planning in order to achieve balanced growth. It supplies the frame of reference for making choices and a focus for the development of facilities and capabilities. Thus planning means a scheme for accomplishing a purpose made beforehand. Plan also refers line of conduct, to be taken for the development of any proposed to make it best out of it. Well-neighed plan is necessary for the development of any scheme.

The planning and development of tourism relate to the natural, cultural and other resources and economic and social environments. While attempting at tourism planning and development it is essential to consider the implications of change for the several environments connecting or holding together and being joined by tourism development. The purpose of planning is to establish a comprehensive scheme in which development of tourism industries can be considered. The policy makers must be concerned with a broad set of economic, social, environmental and geographic effects associated with the trend towards and pressures of growth. The emphasis of tourism development is to help in the decision making and policy setting processes and to assist in developing tourism according to the aspirations and needs of the country.

The development plan for tourism should be to prepare an inventory of the tourist assets in the country. These assets might be classified in three categories—natural attractions, man-made attractions and special events. In preparing items in these categories no feature should be omitted, however insignificant it may seem. Local residents often overlook features which may interest the tourists. This is generally so in the case of man-made attractions. Tourism should capitalize on the unique feature of the country giving special emphasis on the value of history. Generally, people are interested in history, and the site of an old monument, temple or early archaeological ruins will attract tourists if proper arrangement is made to explain precisely about them. Many countries are developing and creating historical museum and these, as well as natural history museums featuring specially the plant and animal life and geology of the country, which provide attraction and interest for the international visitors.

Flora and Fauna reserves and peculiar rare species of plants, flowers and animals are also great attractions.

National parks, wildlife reserves and conservation areas can become great tourist attractions if suitably managed and presented. Side by side with natural attractions, the historic monuments, religious shrines, stupas, temples and traditional environment must be up-kept for a visit by tourists and residents alike. But only reknown historic monuments and prominent religious places receive attention of the authorities. In this regard, many other equally famous examples of indigenous architecture which are unnoticed and left to deteriorate could be utilized for tourism use if proper care is taken and used while making tourism planning and development. So the creation of integrated environment on a reasonable and intimate design could bring substantial benefits, both for material and cultural advancement. If properly planned, such environment should attract tourists in large numbers. The tourism plans needing for building works, infrastructures or interference with the landscape must be in keeping with the needs and the economic, social and financial potential of the local residents. The integrated planning of all transport and economic structures and the sheltering environmental protection measures should be adjusted properly not to be unmatching to the site. The Planning concepts of development, socio-cultural environmental factors must be based on zoning and to be reckoned within the development strategy which is also clearly put in the planning. It also identifies market areas with best potential. Such schemes if included in the tourism planning, it never causes the pollution of environment on which they build themselves. Tourism seeks attractive environment and natural scenery. Construction and development of hotels, camping sites, parking spaces, gas stations, highways and other tourist facilities should not be used for the reduction of the attractiveness of natural resources.

The check-list for development of tourism must cover by a planning for the following items:—

Accessibility—Improvement of highways, construction of bridges, turn-arounds, parking lots, signposting, mileage and route indicators. Road maps, the place names, water supply, toilet facilities, shelter places, lookouts, camping and caravan areas should be made at right places for the convenience of the tourists. The development of basic tourist resources whether given by nature or whether the result of the activities of man cannot be brought about except by means of accessibility. Accessibility permits visitors to come to the place for seeing objects of attraction. The demand relates to means of transport in the place of attractions in a well-defined time is generally necessity and this is possible only by means of accessibility of road. Accessibility makes tourist movement favourable in the places of attractions for which the network of road is becoming more and more for motor tourism. Accessibility is must for the utilization of tourist resources.

Scenery Preservation—The planning scheme must posses beaches with clean, wide, soft sand, free of pollution, mountains, picturesque and colourful or suitable for skiing or trekking; flora and fauna attractive and of many varieties.

Climate—Rainfall/warmth-cold—the seasonal periods and it is short or of long duration. It would be noticed whether the visitor be affected or inconvenienced by the climate.

Geophysical Features—These features offer variety and develop interest among the tourist. If there are waterfalls, natural and artificial lakes, these are to be presented in the best possible ways. The inland waterways, rivers, streams, canals, georges etc. are to be featured and listed with all details.

Side by side with natural resources, historical, cultural and human resources should be listed in the planning with identification and of all historical, cultural and human resources with due consideration. Measures should be taken to encourage the local culture in the planning with intention of benefit of the residents and the tourist alike. Due consideration in planning should be given to all manifestations of culture not only those regarded as exceptional but also the less attractive. Every thought to be given for the use of historic buildings as hotels, restaurants and souvenir shops which should contribute to their preservation. As far as possible, the use of traditional architecture should be utilized in building tourist facilities in the planning. Unique cultural assets compose of the cultural and natural property of the country. In being partly hold on such cultural and natural attractions, tourism may also contribute a role in preserving and developing them. Assessing tourist potential, scenery preservation plays a leading role and should be undertaken consciously and methodically and carefully planned as part of the national development effort. The most important aspect is that care should be taken to identify the real tourism product or products which the country has in its fold and likes to develop them in the tourism planning. While capitalizing such unique products of the country in order to make maximum use of local resources, to ensure a marketable product and to lessen risk of competition from other destinations. In order to maintain scenery preservation—conservation and regeneration of native flora, roadside planting, rubbish and weed removal, preservation of historical relics, runs and upkeepment of religious temples, shrines and pilgrimage sites should be properly done and executed. Side by side with them care of monuments, parks and gardens, recognition of native flora and fauna, geological formations etc. should be maintained and preserved for development.

The Development Projects for tourism should include these items as construction of parks, open areas, toilet facilities, swimming pools, car parks. Encouragement should also be given for construction and improvement of hotels, guest houses, restaurants and camping sites. There is also need for inclusion of facilities for fostering the establishment of entertainment, recreation and amusement for visitors. Provision should also be made for establishment of art galleries, museums, libraries and exhibitions of local handicrafts and industries. By making tourism development project, with the above objectives in view, it can make a substantial contribution to the economic and social development of the country. Only those tourist facilities and accommodations of sufficient scale and with affirmed profitability should be endorsed on the development projects for tourism. All newly constructed enterprises should have strong aesthetic appeal and high quality service to visitors so that they can improve, rather than deteriorate the appeal of the land to tourists.

The tourism plan for development must take notice on transport facilities. The accessibility is the prime concern for tourism development, so the improvement of road, rail and air services and terminal facilities must be adjusted to cope the visitor's flow and properly managed to their services. Improvement of taxi and hire car services, boating services in the lakes, coach tours and special tourist flights must also be taken into consideration for making development projects for tourism.

Having prepared all above items of tourism plan, the next approach is to determine ways and means for getting the work accomplished. Many of the items specified would be within the sphere of regional administration and these could be submitted to the districts concerned. Other items would concern Central Administration or National Government and its various ministries and departments as the main agencies which could be approached in respect of these works. Community or local co-operation would be a necessity. As tourism thrives on hospitality and so the people must be helpful and gentle while dealing with the international tourists. Many private industry-oriented organisations has been created and they have done a reasonable good job of serving the visitors. But such private organisations should try to regulate the industry (tourism) to fully ensure that not only are tourists are well-served, but also the life of the indigenous culture preserved. This can be achieved easily if the activities of the government organisations and the support given to it by the local residents will encourage private interests to undertake improvements and new developments. Short-term programme for tourism development would be desirable than a comprehensive development plan, as it could take years to implement. Short-term plan could be completed in short period and this in turn would lead to greater community support for the remainder of the development programme.

The devising of a development plan is important, but it can break down and fail if each item mentioned above is not carefully recorded and faithfully followed up.

Tourism is a luxury export consumed by international visitors as non-citizens in the exporting (not in importing) country. Many of the social, cultural and political consequences of tourism flow from its being an internally consumed export. The emphasis is to be made on political and economic issues with special reference to the organisation and planning of the tourism sector in the context of the overall goals of national development. As we have noticed that tourism development would cause the multiplier effect by earning foreign exchange which is redistributed to other branches of national economy. Development of the country infrastructure is sure to assist in a general economic improvement of benefit to all the inhabitants. The necessity of setting clear objectives in tourism planning needs to be a real concern for the incidence of gains and losses within the community and the nature of the social impacts. There should not be any problem of the impact on the quality of the environment and the satisfaction of tourists.

10

TOURISM PROMOTION AND PUBLICITY

International Tourism became an organised trade product only in the early 1960's. It now is regarded as an export oriented industry. Many countries now are viering to develop and to claim for a fair share of the international markets purchasing the product. Tourism is an expanding industry. Throughout the world there is a growing recognition of the importance of the tourist industry. It is the main source of foreign exchange and an important factor in the development of industry and international trade for many countries. With the development of speedy and aggressive growth of cheaper long distance travel through the efforts of airlines and destination areas of tourism development the tourism product is brought within the easy reach of the average income bracket customer causing in new markets being developed for the same product.

The promotion plan signifies two major questions :

(*a*) What have the country to sell?
(*b*) Where is the market?

The answer to the first question will generally be found in the inventory of tourist assets prepared for tourism development by the country. Every country may not have outstanding attractions such as snowy mountains, lakes, serene landscapes but a careful appraisal of its tourist attractions should bring out the features which would be the main selling points.

For an answer to the second question it would be were to

meet the tourists who had already travelled the area. Find out where they come from, why they come, when they come. This information might be collected from local sources, but if not available a questionnaire could be prepared and visitors could be invited to complete it when leaving. While going through the answers from the visitors a questionnaire will atleast point to the particular field of market of any country interested in the development of travel trade. This also will provide the kind of visitors interested in the country and what attracts them. This will provide with a basis on which to develop a promotion campaign. A good promotion campaign will tell the full account of any country's attractions to the potential visitor. It will also provide for advertising and publicity through all practicable media, *e.g.*, free literature, press advertising, radio, television, films, direct mail etc.

The scale on which this programme is to be carried will depend upon available resources of labour and fund. The launching for publicity and the development of a comprehensive advertising programme call for skill and enterprise and the employment of a qualified publicity or public relations officer, for this work should help and assist in increased tourist business.

While preparing a tourist promotion and publicity plan for any country, it is essential to let the local residents (people) in that country know the plans for development of tourism in order to secure their support. Without which this it cannot flourish. This can be done by radio and television interviews and news releases to the local press.

It is also important to gain local recognition of the necessity for spending outside the country the money provided for country's promotion campaign in order to reach the desired tourist market.

The essential item in any promotion campaign is the brochure. Brochure may be promotional or informative. The promotional brochure is usually illustrated in colour, printed on high quality paper and contains authentic descriptions. Its main purpose is to arouse interest and create a desire to visit.

Tourism Publicity, in general terms, means the act of bringing common knowledge to public attention. So the ultimate purpose of tourism publicity is to increase the number of visitors to any one area. Where the publicity is generated by the National Tourist Organisation, travel agents or the chamber of commerce, it concerns little to the promoter by which means the tourist travels or at which hotel or guest house he stays. The promoters have achieved their aim by the tourist's presence in their area. Where the promoter is a carrier, hotel proprietor, supplier of a service, however the purpose of his publicity is to induce the tourist to buy the tickets, tours and services offered by the promoter in the advertisement or described in the publicity.

Tourism is an industry in which abstract nature of the commodity is to be sold, *i.e.* beautiful natural scenery, atmosphere, landscape, surroundings, relaxation, snow, mountain, sunshine etc. So it is difficult to prepare material in a plane which is conducive to tourist mind. These psychological investigations are the targets at which tourist publicity must aim for tourist attraction. The ultimate purpose of tourist publicity is to increase the number of tourists to any one area.

It is not out of place to define propaganda which sometimes is considered as part of publicity. Propaganda is generally used with a deciduous connotation and is not concerned with the exact and authentic narration but rather seeking every means to drug their awareness and suspend the operation of their intellects. Propaganda should be excluded from economic activities and limited to political activity.

Publicity, in the narrow sense means specific editorial material and information concerning certain goods and services written in such a way that the newspaper or magazine publicises it free of charge because it will be interesting to its readers (Advertising is paid for and space is limited). In a wider sense, publicity is the group of complementary efforts which aims to spread an idea and sell a product.

Now-a-days, publicity and propaganda are only part of the whole promotional campaign in which public relations and marketing also play important roles.

Tourism is involved in the pursuit of economic industry. It is acclaimed as invisible export. So the developing countries of the world are earning a measure of foreign currency out of tourism. In order to earn more foreign currency a measure for the development and promotion of tourism should be done. Such promotional and publicity activities in other words, aim at the improvement of invisible export. The good and sound publicity has a direct leaning with receipts from tourism. It makes easy receipt with the influx of large number of tourists. It provides involvement for the increase of capacity of transportation and for the protection of touristic resources and promotion of uses. Propaganda is generally attached with an aim to attract crowd or mass for the gain of the few. It has no purpose for the gain of those who support its propaganda thrives on exaggeration and not on reality. It is important, when planning tourist publicity, to consider that tourists make their choice of holidays in as rational a manner as they choose other things important to them.

While choosing the strategy, its aim is bound up with the role assigned to General Economic Policy and must be a part and parcel of the country's tourist resources and plant. The choice of tourist publicity depends on the tourist resources. The abundance or scarcity of basic tourist resources which by its very definition implies their development. The followings items are very important:—

Climate—Tourists prefer hot and dry or Mediterranean type of climate and not cold damp climate.

Attractions—Scenery, coast, valleys, island, mountains, desert etc. is often utilized as a publicity argument. Natural beauty can be found in some exceptional situation or in a quiet countryside, in a lake or seashore, on mountain peaks or in crayons. These also help local development.

Accessibility—The publicity can be of no use by publicising a district difficult to access. Importance of roads and communications plays a vital part in making publicity. The district having attractive natural resources cannot be focus lacking accessibility.

Man-made attractions deserve publicity. Architecture, historic monuments and artistic treasures are permanent attractions and all kinds of cultural events such as festivals, religious events, sporting, folklore are periodical attractions are all to be subject of focus for publicity.

Strategy for publicity must take into consideration objectives and the budget. It depends upon every country's economic policy, which aspires implicitly or explicitly to bring the maximum returns and even then there must be a system of priorities. The following choices must be made in advance—

What type of tourism to be developed? International or Domestic? Tourism for the young or for aged persons? Whether publicity be focussed on regions already popular or an new areas—economically backward? Establishment of priorities helps much for ensuring effective publicity.

Government as well as travel trade people must contribute reasonable budget or money for publicity. If the contribution of money is less or say 1 per cent of the total tourist receipt, the publicity strategy must be more modest. It is not good to be over ambitious, objectives for publicity campaign out of insufficient financial resources which cause less favourable result.

The publicity programme will differ from country to country. In a democratic and free country, the government will initiate and co-ordinate activities while publicity will be mainly the field of private sector.

Publicity strategy will also be affected by the legal and administrative system of the country.

The publicity campaign should be useful when it is co-ordinated with infrastructural development. It is not useful to copy the publicity of the competitor's model but must be based or carried objectively, keeping eye on the factors of the national services and resources. Lastly, more care should be taken for irrational reactions and psychological factors.

Activities of National Tourist Offices abroad are created by the governments of the concerned countries which are entrusted with the works as the representatives. They have offices in foreign country's capitals and other large cities in the main tourist-generating countries. Tourism publicity plays an important role in shaping the efficiency of Tourism Administration. Tourism Administration is a part and parcel of tourism publicity. Tourists are attracted to visit the country when they see the reality in advertising an in various tourist materials. The overseas office acts as an Information Bureau where advice is given in verbal ways and the visitors come to call in the office, supply advice in answer by telephone and better inquiries. These offices distribute printed publicity material as brochures, folders, information leaflets, posters and films from the country concerned. These offices will have a budget for its publicity campaign which will help them to give advertisements in the Newspapers and magazines. newspapers, television and radio and film reporters are the overseas tourist office's special outlets. In reality, the overseas tourist offices are regarded as vital centres for public relations. It is the work of public relations to build up a friendly attitude towards the country seeking tourists and as such public relations is one of the very first concern of the overseas Tourist offices. The public relation concern and works through selected outlets and not as publicity of mass appeal. Public relations men also approach special type of peoples to their influence such as civil servants, teachers, sportsmen, businessmen etc. and able to organise, special tour for them in the countries concerned. They also arrange seminars, field trips, conventions, and conferences and special receptions in the country concerned. They must be looked for individual contacts as well as the group contact. Reliability of the information of the public relation men must be clear and true and it should not be a false representation nor a exaggeration. They have not to supply propaganda or incorrect pushing of informations.

The characteristic of the publicity between the enterprises and tourism has different one. Expenses of the tourism cover up the whole area of the famous places of the country as their profitable margin. They extend to wide areas so that their need government has to subsidize. Again National Tourist Organisation has a closer link with all sorts of organisations. It must have co-ordination and co-operation with all government departments, private organisations, business concerns, associations and others. All these are related with tourism in one or other ways as these associate aims with tourism as their purpose. The main tourist will is publicity which in turn means receipts. Tourist publicity is one of Government's duties, even though it is often aided by private organisations, transportation, hotels, and entertainment centres and airlines. Tourists publicity involves, therefore, the formulation of a programme, prepared by the responsible public services. But the main, basic theme on a national scale is concerned by the National Tourist Organisation. Unlike National Tourist offices, private profit-making tourist organisations are specially concerned with selling holidays and travel. They also present the image of a country popular for holidays but they will be much more intimately concerned with building up the economic importance of tourism. These private organisations put accent on the special image they offer.

The methods and techniques of publicity, activity as said before, depend on policy-making so far as a country is concerned and in the case of a private organisation, its commercial policy. Both of them have their own definition of objectives concerning the resources and supply of services available. The preparation of an overall publicity strategy must be based on a knowledge of the market. Strategy implies the selection of the most effective means and their application to winning the competitive battle for tourists. It is concerned with the most profitable use of the publicity budget to increase the number of tourists, overnight stays etc. and receive increased foreign exchange from tourism. To plan good publicity with successful results, market studies and operational research have been regarded as the basic instrument in its broadest sense. These studies and researches are supply and demand elements of tourist market which will help to harmonise development by adjusting as to avoid imbalance. Such synthesis helps to overall relation between the product or service and its present and future, actual and potential consumers.

11

MARKETING OF TOURISM

Marketing Techniques

Marketing means a set of techniques for substantiating existing products on the market. Present marketing techniques attach the importance of adopting the product or service to customer requirements. The product or service may be present or potential. So in order to approach a marketing, a through understanding of the market and motivations is necessary for tourism. Marketing, with its centre on identification of market, product planning and communication, is a domain in which many tourism issues and great future potential exist. Identification of market segments by employing such techniques as benefit fragment and development of traveller motive profiles is considered to be the first measure in improving both product and promotion. The surveys and inquiries utilize for planning publicity and advertisement are equally useful for marketing.

A tourism industry is made up of a whole host of activities and industries, directly or indirectly affected by it to varying degrees. The market investigation in tourism which is necessitated to identify the individual consumer's ends and to quantify them by market segments is, as always concerned with the characteristics of the holidays which tourists are interested to buy. The chief characteristics and motivations of the potential market aims to enter, develop and promote by adopting and or creating tourist products and services to meet its requirements. In this regard the types of movements of tourists to be accounted, as for example those who travel by choice for holiday, leisure and recreation and those who travel for mandatory reasons as business, family, missions etc. These two types of movements must be considered on an international level (short-haul and long-haul) as well as on a national level. The following factors are to be known for making marketing approach in tourism:-

— Introduction to marketing principles.
— Development of marketing objectives and development of the Marketing Strategy.
— Preparing a marketing plan, testing and monitoring.
— Marketing organisation.
— Budgeting and Revenue Raising.

Marketing Principles

In order to develop the market it is essential to know what will the market buy?

For this, product idea development is necessary for new products and products idea assessment. New product needs testing. As for existing products, examination of producer's sales idea is very important by surveys at the point of sale or surveys among consumers. These two product idea assessments, help much in understanding potential tourists in the generating country and identifying target groups. They also assist in finding ways for communication with target groups, and delivering the products.

Marketing Objectives

While most countries are in favour of developing tourism and the development of marketing objectives and strategy can only be formulated in the context of each country's overall policies and objectives for tourism which must point to the benefits sought from tourism and its capacity for receiving tourists takingness. Objectives should envisage the prime potential market groups in selected tourism generating countries, their size and characteristics and an undertaking should be made to set down the numbers of tourists to be attracted from these groups, their expected spending capacity and the seasonal pattern of their arrival.

Marketing Strategy

The marketing strategy should view the means whereby the potential market groups are to be attracted, informed and the measure whereby the product is to be acquired by them or delivered to them. To use marketing strategy, the people responsible for it should choose from among the many communication media available to those that can reach the potential market most cost effectively. The product strategy and the Product Mix should be created by making assets register, with ratings of competitive attractions, is an essential starting point. The Product Mix which will be evolved from the assets will depend upon the nature of those assets and the extent to which they can be diversified. The mere fact that the consumer has to be taken to the point-of-supply changes the whole relationship as between producer, wholesaler and retailer.

As a general rule, the tourism industry uses the most conventional marketing channel, containing two marketing intermediaries—a wholesaler and a retailer. The wholesaler, typically, is the middleman who will package combinations of tourism products, assembling the product lines of many producers into unique assortments to match different segments of demand on a scale which will meet these demands and he will stimulate exchanges. Also, typically, he will sell to the consumers through retailers, the Travel Agents. He will also need to choose and work with and motivate interests such as travel agents whose ultimate task it will be to arrange for the product to be delivered to the consumer. Communication Mix also will create awareness and use which will stimulate word-of-mouth promotion, will supplement (and possibly replace) other promotional efforts.

The Transaction Mix is necessary as a National Tourist Organisation cannot be so concerned in the commercial mechanism of transfer of title. But it can and should be vitally concerned with those pre and post-sale services which will help the tourist to make and subsequently approve his purchase decision. So it must be now realized that communication is the body on the framework of market cultivation. It embraces all information flows. It is not just advertising, as is commonly thought. So the main media available for communication are as follows: Newspapers, general interest magazines, specialised magazines, television, radio, cinema, posters, brochures, mail drop, consultation on lecture tours, stands at exhibition and fairs, cultural and artistic events, invitations extended to opinion leaders, journalists etc. and tourism fairs and exchanges for reaching the trade.

Marketing Plan : Preparing, Testing and Monitoring

The idea of the potential market on target group is followed. The technique of attracting target group will be arranged through the 'profile' of a typical potential customer in terms of age, income, social status, educational level, previous travel experience, travel aspirations etc. The target group to which any country or countries may realistically address his/their marketing and it is all the more important therefore to find methods of reaching these efficiently and to minimize wastage and loss. When the target group is identified, the next step will be to devise a message to address it and to select the best medium for reaching it cost effectively with the ultimate aim of attracting and convincing at least some members of the group to make a purchase.

Here it is very important to identify and study the role of competitors, before deciding on the message. The most outstanding competitors are those supplying broadly similar attractions to the tourist within about the same price range. The role of prices of a tourism product likely to be an unprecise affair since the product can be made up of so many elements that are each affected by their own individual pricing policy. However, this does not apply when individual products are put together into a package, pricing of which is under the direct control of the consolidator. As for example, a hotel quotes a room-rate which includes all meals, use of the swimming-pool, membership of its casino club and so on.

However, precise or imprecise the pricing may be, it will or should arise from consideration of defined objectives. Firstly, there is that of market penetration when the prices are set deliberately low to stimulate market growth and to capture a large share of it. The practice is particularly applicable to the highly price-sensitive markets where many new consumers would be attracted to the market if the product was priced low enough. Such a low price would also discourage competition.

It is common practice for the message to be in two parts to convey ,

(a) reassurance that the satisfaction sought by the customer can be provided, and

(b) that the product offered something extra that the competitors could not *i.e.* the USP or Unique Sales Point.

There is a demonstration with discussion of advertisements produced for a variety of countries, airlines and tour operations showing how each is majored on its USP.

Regarding choice of medium, there is a demonstration of the sophisticated analysis of readerships and audiences of press and other media available in generating countries.

Travel was an ancient industry and honourable business and not just a phenomenon of the present world. But many of the National Tourist Organisations so far have not been able to develop professionalism in marketing. The personnels attached with overseas offices of the National Tourist Organisations principally are not satisfactorily familiar with the fundamentals of the travel industry and were never entrusted before with marketing responsibilities. Therefore, to have proper marketing in tourism, is to acquaint the marketing personnels in the technique and fulfilment of their marketing responsibilities. Many attach the main obstacle in the way of proper marketing the lack of funds. But the main lack is of acquaintance with the product for selling and shortage of marketing experience. It is the need of the hour, that all marketing personnels attached with the National Tourist Organisations should be required to undergo formal training in regular courses.

The lack of knowledge of what motivates people to travel? In order to make the right marketing strategy, it is important to get to know the psychology of the visitor and the prospects. So there is always the need for research. Here a distinction should be made between research and statistics. No doubt, statistics are very important as an aid to find a total marketing programme but they generally take long time in compiling datas causing them ineffective as marketing tool. Statistics could be misleading, unless carefully analysed. But the interviews with visitors based on statistical type research should be carried on at the destination as well as in the country of origin after their return to the home country.

Research supported by detailed and reliable studies is very costly. It would, therefore, be aimed at to make co-operative endeavour with enterprises such as airlines, travel trade associations, publishes and other related industries and start studies on analytical ways. The problem of quantifying demand is of special importance to the tourism industry where big capital investment is often at danger. The National Tourist Organisation firstly must know how many visitors will be visiting the country in the coming years, essentially for five years, the markets which will generate them; and the purposes of their visits. Forecasting in the tourism industry is laden with difficulties concurring no more so than in other industries. The chief factors tending to these obstacles are the complex nature of the tourism product and the wide series of motivations which produce consumer demand.

Subjective forecasting consisting of the projection, intuition, judgement and insight etc. has an important role to play in the tourism industry where forecasts so often have to be subjected to such unforeseen influences as social and political changes in both the major tourist generating countries and in the destination areas. More so, there are several factors in tourism which are always changing and which can make a mistake of the assumption—new air fares, government policy towards charter flights, government attitude and participation in the destination country and so on.

Sometime international comparison by the use of analogies is occasionally used such as the antithesis produced by an aircraft manufacturer on charter inclusive tours.

Economic Models are becoming increasingly popular in the tourism industry. Tipical of the variables that are being used are the following:-

- — fares
- — quality of air travel
- — average expenditure per trip.
- — availability of leisure time.
- — population
- — economic indicators (investment, savings, trade, GNP etc.)

A useful discipline for managements, ahead of a decision to invest in a given campaign or following the models of marketing is to set down the available budget ready at hand, the minimum acceptable return and the number of sales to be made to achieve it. It is here better to follow the way usually major tour operators do this. It is known to all that mass communication exercises, sophisticated data used in planning big budget are not near at hand for smaller operations and public relation activities. But some quantitative indications can generally be gathered and the same thought processes can be applied to planning, targeting and testing.

Marketing is considered to be not an exact science but rather a craft which has to be learned to a certain extent by experience and self-monitoring. The analysis, predictions and assessments based on formal and informal research can be used before the campaign starts, but there can be no real guarantee of success. It is advised that before starting into heavy promotional investments, carry out firstly the small scale test campaign and pilot exercises. These techniques help to reduce the risk factor. Stress should be made on the system-approach in designing a marketing programme. The system approach should commence with the headquarter of the National Tourist Organisation and extend through the field operations. It should include fixing of priorities and deadlines, back-up services and reporting procedures. The importance of individuals must not be forgotten while doing marketing programme. Many National Tourism Organisations are inclined to design their marketing programme joining hand with carriers, tour operators and retail travel agents and so the marketing officers do not possess the necessary professionalism nor are given sufficient budget to work. The individual should be the principal target, though the growth of group traffic is increasing because the group ultimately consists of individuals. To do advertising and promotion in consumer magazines costs a lot which the National Tourism Organisations cannot venture for them due to meagre funds available to them. So it is advisable to undertake organised Public Relations. Public Relation is expensive in terms of time but can accomplish satisfactory and glorious results if intelligently applied in tourism marketing. But public relation thrives on a continuous flow of information to the media which is only possible if National Tourism Organisation establish a system of information gathering and feeding the media through their overseas offices and public relation agencies. The decision making procedure should be simple, clear and at times to facilitate implementation. Quick decision helps much to fulfil the gap between the producer or servicing agent and the consumer.

12

HOSPITALITY AND TOURISM

The State creates the general infrastructures essential for tourism. The importance of tourism in the national economy is very great. The contribution of tourism exceeds that of other sectors in several countries, to the extent that it appears as one of the essential elements in the Balance ofTrade. Tourism is generally a fast expanding sector, the future importance of which is very glorious. In fact, tourism depends to a large extent on the public utility infrastructures. There is no doubt that certain public services play a leading role in its development. A country wishing to receive tourists must give them the best of receptions by making available the necessary public services (customs, roads, car-parts, beaches, health services, security services, parts, airports, post and telephones etc.). These services must, as far as possible, be of the best quality. Even if the public infrastructures have not been created for purely tourist purposes they are obviously used by the tourists and their smooth running is fundamental for the country's tourist reputation. In any case, economic activity benefits from the existence of the correct infrastructure, especially in the new countries which desire to increase the value of their tourist resources.

The State also provides specialized equipments for tourism development. Side by side with the creation of specialised equipments, the state is responsible for preservation and opening up of cultural amenities. Another sector where the presence of the state planning is necessary is that of Vocational Training (Technical or advanced). The quality of tourist services depends not only on the excellence of the installations and general infrastructures but also on the quality of personal services. The state, therefore, must ensure that there is the necessary vocational training. Private schools must be established which may train chefs, guides, tourist office staff, hostesses, ski, sailing instructors. The diplomas must be officially awarded by the state, ratifying the qualifications. International recognition of the diplomas awarded by each country is also to be considered.

Hospitality and tourism for development provides an opportunity for progressive industrial/human relations to be developed. There is a growing interest in the present world in managing tourism development in order to optimize its benefits and determents. Tourism needs the most effective use of productive resources, so there is need of technical programme in the field of hotel, catering and Tourism. Tourist industry is a service-oriented industry, so human resources need for personnel and professional power for catering sound services. Tourism is a labour intensive 'People Oriented' industry. As such, its success depends heavily on the availability of a high quality and committed workforce. There is need to integrate labour demand planning in tourism into overall strategic planning of the workforce efforts in both the public and private sector. There must be provision for human investment to improve productivity. An enhanced development of the human resource base in tourism through education and training must be made by establishing proper training institutes. The objectives of such training institutes should be based on the following intentions :

- Provide a greater overall priority to sound and effective tourism education and training programmes at all levels.
- Give impetus to all sectors of the tourism industry to keenly co-operate in the development of training and education programme to assure that training meets the needs of a diverse workforce.
- Cherish the training, education and placement of indigenous management and workers.

Hospitality services offered in an authentic manner on a business basis will provide quality and profit. Professionalism in the hospitality industry will continue to expand, attracting a new generation of professionals committed to the belief of services to the tourists deriving both financial and psychological gains from their work. Tourism offers investment opportunities ; the possibility of creating jobs utilising the labour force. Tourism offers new opportunities for employment. Tourism can offer new opportunities in employment and in entrepreneurship.

Under proper planning conditions, tourism may also provide an impetus to social change directly through education and training to meet the needs of a service industry and indirectly by introducing different social habits and patterns. Hospitality and civic sense in people is key to the development of tourism. Many people do not know the advantages and disadvantages created by touristic development. But people of the country should fully know what it is and they should be aware of their duty and hospitality. The lasting impression of international visitors could have, is all the behaviour and hospitality of the country towards. Therefore, the government of the countries should communicate these things to the people in general. Tourism has secondary spillover effects in other sectors. Through increased demand for foodstuffs, souvenirs and other goods, it generates employment in agriculture, food processing, handicrafts and light manufacturing. Jobs also will be created when new hotels and tourist area developments are built. These establishments and infrastructures need skilled manpower to man and manage these activities. So the special faculties or schools and other service training institutes are needed for the local people for improving the skills of the host population for jobs in tourism. The indirect employment generated by tourism spreads out more widely into the local people and must be considered, as well as direct employment in evaluating tourism. More planning is required to ensure that residents of local area can qualify for job opportunities that tourism created sence without training in the local area. Such jobs tend to go to people for major urban areas.

Tourism needs a large number of personal services, which would be delicate to mechanise or automate. Employment manpower and staff problems are very important since big and costly tourist plant cannot be managed without qualified staff. Employment and Vocational training, therefore, constitute part of tourist supply.

Tourism creates jobs directly and indirectly. By inducing various economic activities, the expansion of tourism provides employment opportunities in the occupations directly connected with tourism as well as other branches of activity indirectly involved. In order to get more, it may be useful to note the following :

- Tourism provides a new flow for local foodstuffs; *i.e.* for agricultural crops, including processed products (wine, cheese, salt provisions). This is acquired by the phenomenon of 'Consumption transfers.'
- Tourism may supply secondary and seasonal employment for agricultural workers *e.g.* jobs at tourist season in tourist resorts where there will be a mass flow of tourists.
- The handicrafts furnish in tourism good outlet for their products. Souvenir made of wood, bronze, copper, wicker, the sale of lace, pottery, local articles made of straw, leather textiles, handmade carpets etc. Many artisans are occupied in souvenir productions and so receive remunerative occupation.
- Tourism and industry are inter-dependent not only in the opening stage or construction stage of building and fitting up hotel plant but also for the aptness of supplementary equipment for communications and transport. Industry supplies tourism with railway carriages, coaches, cars and buses and aircraft for transport, with lifts, kitchen equipments, shutters and locking apparatus for hotels together with sports equipments, bulk of cement, glass, textiles and concrete.
- All commercial enterprises participate and go in the rear to a large degree in tourism activities.

Tourism, being a service industry, vocational training is a

necessity. The personnel working in tourism particularly in hotels, travel agencies and reception offices are to be properly trained and qualified. They must adept in technical know-how alongwith personal potentialities such as amiability, quick instruction, tact, balance, self-control, contemplative direction and ready witted manners, ready conversation, insight and more a knowledge of the customs, habits, tastes and rules of conduct of foreign tourists.

Side by side, the above qualifications, the need for a practical knowledge of foreign languages is a necessity. Many countries have established an official classification of the various tourist occupations. But the systems, categories and terminology differ from one country to another.

Advance Vocational Training in Tourism (for executives) is given in a number of universities, economic institutes and advance business schools.

Each year at Turin (Toreno), North Italy, the International Centre for Advance Tourism Studies set up by International Union of Official Travel Organisations (IUOTO) is providing a cycle of advance studies for persons who already have professional experience in tourism.

Many advanced countries in the world have established Hotel and Restaurant Administration for providing regular courses of touring/educational opportunities to the people interested in these courses. These courses cover Certificate in Hospitality and Tourism (one year), specialized three or four year course in Hotel and Restaurant Management etc. So, there is availability of a full range of training/educational opportunities in the advanced countries in the world.

Hospitality and Tourism are closely related with each other. The public utility infrastructures are also closely linked up with tourism to a large extent. So the smooth working of certain public services play an extra-ordinary role in the development of tourism. *Firstly*, the state must provide the avenues of best of receptions by making available the necessary public services *e.g.* customs, roads, car-parks, health centres, security services, airports, post and telegraph and telephones etc. These services must be managed and looked after by well-trained officers and personnels who are proficient in technical and professional knowledge of the subjects as well as representation of amiable manners and dealings while communicating with the foreign visitors. Indeed, as tourist industry expands, the services of government officers or public utility services will become increasingly important. Actually, these officers are really the pillars who actually stimulate the flow of tourist traffic in the country by properly dealing with them in a more lovable manner. With the increase in tourist services, the standard of facilities has to be improved with the amicable manners of the officers who are in-charge of utility services in the standard suitable to be accepted by international tourists. Similarly, the public and private travel trade organisations must try to create tourist satisfaction by the provision of high quality human environments. Favourable hospitality and lovable dealings of the persons associated with the international tourist in hotels or travel agencies or other travel organisations can result in repeat visits of international tourists. So the hotels and travel agencies cannot operate without persons able to perform competent services. Exerting an active services, these service agencies must ensure first-rate and meet the requirements of tourist traffic.

There are certain segments of activity which only a state or government could take care of. This is so even in most advanced countries. The management of airports—both international and domestic and their development is a continuous process and costly one too. The aero-engine technical improvements (the Jumbo Jets-Air buses) are carrying a large number of passengers. So looking at the feasible and actually under-development process, it is now time for any country wishing to receive influx of international tourists, to plan in advance for bringing up ground-handling facilities at the airports and fully skilled man-power to man and manage them.

BIBLIOGRAPHY

1. *Ed.* Donald E. Hawkins, Elwood L. Shafer, James M. Rovelsfad, *Tourism Planning and Development Issues,* George Washington University, Washington D.C. 1980.
2. *Ed.* Donald E. Hawkins, Elwood L. Shafer, James M. Rovelsfad, *Tourism Marketing and Management Issues,* George Washington University, Washington D.C., 1980.
3. Emanuel de Kadt, *Tourism, Passport to Development?* A Joint World Bank—UNESCO. Study 1979.
4. Brydeu, John M. —*Tourism and Development.* Cambridge University Press, Cambridge, 1973.
5. Sasser W. Earl, R. Paul Olsen, and D. Daryl Wyckoff. *Management of Service Operations,* Allyn and Bacon Inc., Boston 1978.
6. Training of Tourism Office Personnel: *The Role and Functions of a National Tourism Office Abroad,* 1976, Geneva.
7. A.K. Bhatia : *Tourism Development, Principles and Practice*—Sterling Publishers, New Delhi, India, 1995.
8. Nash, Dennison : *Anthropology of Tourism,* Pergamon, 1996.
9. Pye, E, and I.B. Lin : *Tourism in Asia : The Economic Impact.* Singapore University Press, 1983.

INDEX